Mechanicsville:

A Test of Loyalty

Laurie Stewart

Mechanicsville: A Test of Loyalty

Mechanicsville: A Test of Loyalty

Mechanicsville: A Test of Loyalty

Mechanicsville: A Test of Loyalty

For my mom, who always believed
I could do it.

For the love of my life, Jim, for giving me the courage to do
it.

For all my friends, who kept bugging me to do it.

This one's for you.

Laurie Stewart, 2015

Mechanicsville: A Test of Loyalty

CHAPTER ONE
Beginnings

Samantha

We moved on a Saturday in late August. I hated the place from the moment the U-Haul pulled up. I couldn't believe how filthy it was; there was graffiti everywhere, even on the steps. At the bottom, they sunk into the ground leaving a quarter step on one side and a half on the other. I imagined they kept going down past the ground all the way to hell.

The nightmare continued when my Mom and I went up to see the apartment. It took up half the second floor but the layout was shitty. I mean, there were two doors, but both opened into the same hall, one near each of the stairwells. If the hall was ever on fire, we were screwed.

Mom started looking at the kitchen and I could hear her muttering about how dirty everything was. You could tell that the last people living there didn't clean anything before they left. I'm not even sure they *ever* cleaned the bathroom. It was too gross for words. I decided that if Mom wanted me to clean it, I wanted one of those contamination suits and a flamethrower.

Just across the hall was the door to what was to be my room. It was way too small; I didn't think I could fit in half my stuff. I just wanted to cry, why did everything have to go wrong just as I started the last year of school? It was supposed to be my best year, a senior, maybe on the student council, maybe Prom Queen. Instead I was stuck in a ghetto, well, as close as Ottawa gets to one, anyway.

It started two months ago, when Dad lost his job at some investment firm. He was a manager of some sort. I tried asking what he did once and he talked for an hour trying to explain it to me. At the end I still had no idea. Maybe if he could communicate better, then we wouldn't have ended up moving from our house in Rockcliffe, with its in-ground pool, and basement games room, to this dump off Mechanicsville. You can tell by the name that it's not the most prestigious area of town, not even as good as Chinatown or Little Italy. At least they have cool stores and good ethnic restaurants. Mechanicsville just has cruddy bars and street fights and sirens every night. Needless to say, I hate it here. So does Mom. I hear her and Dad fighting sometimes, when they think I'm asleep.

But I was damned if I'd be seen crying when Dad yelled up the stairs at us to start carrying stuff in. "I might be the man of the house, but I'm not going to do it all." I guess he was accepting his *limitations as a human being* or some other excuse he learned from those stupid talk shows. I hated the way he talked after he got fired. He was so weak, so useless. And on the one day we were supposed to make a good impression? It was so embarrassing.

Two hours later, I was hot, tired, dusty and sick to death of
moving. As I trudged down the steps for one more box, a girl
pushed herself off the truck where she'd been lounging. She was
smoking; something I'd rarely seen someone my age do in public.
She had waist length black hair with hot pink streaks, and was
wearing jeans with holes at the knees. But these weren't fashion a
la mode holes; they were more like "I can't afford new jeans"
holes. I don't give a shit for your opinion holes. She was probably
the coolest person I'd ever seen. Forget the Holy Spirit, I had my
Holey Jeans.

A couple of her friends were standing on the sidewalk by the
truck, looking at me like I was a bug under a microscope. And not
a very interesting bug, at that.

"You shouldn't be leaning on the truck, my dad won't like it." I
couldn't believe I just said that. I sounded so geeky. As she stood
up from the truck, she gave me a challenging look that invited a
fight. I figured she could clean the street with me, so I changed my
tone fast.

"Hi. We're just moving in."

The girls rolled their eyes while Holey Jeans just continued
staring. "No shit, Sherlock," she sneered. Behind me I could hear
Dad's footsteps coming toward the door. He'd be out here any
second, and would freak if he saw them touching the rented truck.
He was adamant that we couldn't afford to pay for any repairs, not
the tiniest scratch.

I guess the girls heard him too, because Holey Jeans flicked her still burning cigarette at my face and stepped onto the sidewalk. She curled her lip at my involuntary flinch. Then she leaned in close to me and whispered silkily.

"Watch your step, daddy's girl because if you make a wrong move, I'll cut your pretty face." Not that I needed convincing but one of her crew added, "She's done it before, even did time for assaulting some skank." The smoke-filled air still lingered as the girls moved away. My Dad arrived just as the last of the odour wafted off. He stood beside me, proudly smiling and watched the girls walking away. "Gee, I didn't mean to scare away your new friends, but I'm sure they'll be back." He was grinning as he said this, but I shuddered. I was afraid he was right.

Supper that night was greasy pizza, not like the ones we usually made ourselves, with fresh tomatoes and basil, and Mom's homemade sauce. It came from some corner, hole in the wall place, with a foreign sounding name. What could a guy named Abdul know about pizza anyway?

My mom tried to make the best of it, acting like it was an adventure, but I could see she was unhappy. So could Dad, he kept making stupid jokes, trying to make us laugh. But they all fell flat. Finally, we just went to bed.

I sat in my room, trying not to cry. I missed my friends, I missed my computer; I missed everything about our old house. I hated my

Lad for it, he was feeling bad already, but how could he get fired like that? And calling it "downsizing", and saying it wasn't his fault didn't make it better. He was still out of a job, and then there was that stupid lawsuit. What was he thinking, putting the house up as a retainer on a lawsuit he *might* win?

The next day was, Sunday, we went to the closest church for Mass. Half of the service was in Italian, and I couldn't understand a thing. Mom looked vaguely humiliated; I guess she figured that she should've known it wasn't a regular English speaking church from the name "La Vita de Santa Maria de Conceptione". There were only a couple of other teenagers there, about ninety percent of the people looked to be over ninety years old. And they were all dressed like someone in a movie, the women all in black with scarves over their hair and the men in dark suits and ties. We sure looked out of place, Mom in her favourite pink skirt suit and Dad in a polo shirt and khakis. Me, I just wore a look of acute embarrassment.

Afterwards the priest was waiting on the steps to greet everyone; he seemed very surprised to see us. He started off talking to Dad in what sounded like excited Italian, and then awkwardly switched to English at our befuddled looks. He so genuinely seemed happy to have new parishioners that Dad found himself promising to attend next week as well. And to try to get to the special Mass on Thursday for a Mrs. Bonavista who was in the hospital.

11

We walked up Preston Street looking for a place we could have lunch, and finally settled on a pub. Dad wasn't thrilled to have me in a drinking establishment, but I was fascinated. The beer menu was twice as big as the food menu! Of course, the amount of beer that I was allowed to have was the same as home: none.

The rest of the day was spent trying to fit a four-bedroom house into a two-bedroom apartment. Dad tried to joke that at least he didn't need to set up his office for awhile, but I could see that he was unhappy about it. I couldn't feel sorry for him; I was too busy hating him for doing this to us.

After supper, I went outside for a bit of air. My parents were not fighting. You know, not fighting in that tense, set your teeth on edge, kind of way. I'd had enough of that and just wanted some quiet that wasn't so loud.

I didn't get it. Holey Jeans and her friends were back. They were sharing a beer back and forth. I tried to ease past them nonchalantly, but they shifted just enough to bock my path. Holey jeans finished the bottle with a long swallow, and waved it in a vaguely threatening way in my direction.

"Where are you going, daddy's girl?" The others watched with sly interest to see what I would do.

"Nowhere." How stupid did that sound? Did I sound like I thought they were going nowhere? That this place was nowhere? I had to add, "Just thought I'd look around the neighbourhood."

"You wanna look around this shit-hole? What for, a way out?" The speaker was a wispy looking girl with a vaguely foreign look to her. My mom would've said that she was anorexic but I thought she was beautiful. I couldn't seem to find a word to say to Wispy, so I just shrugged.

Holey Jeans got my attention back with a wave of the empty bottle. It wasn't anywhere near my head but I still flinched. Weak.

"So, what's your name Miss 'too-good-to-be-here?'"

I did feel I was too good for this place, but I wasn't about to admit it. I was scared of her and her street tough friends.

"Samantha... Sam... Sam Hunter." I tried smiling at her, "And what are your names?"

"It don't matter what their names are," Holey Jeans interrupted. "You ain't nothing around here."

That hardly seemed fair, since they knew mine. But I didn't want to visit the emergency room, so I stayed polite, "What's your name, then?" I asked.

"Ashleigh Maracle Grayson," she said in an almost antagonistic way. I wasn't sure how to respond, so she added, "My dad's Mohawk. Got a problem with that?"

"Cool!" was all I said. After all, I really thought it was. Visions of Adam Beach and Dances with Wolves filled my head. That was far more interesting than my white, middle aged, middle class, unemployed father.

"Cool?" Holey Jeans, now Ashleigh asked.

"Yeah, we don't get many Natives where I come from."

"And where do you come from?" Ashleigh leaned into me, obviously threatening violence should I say the wrong thing. I figured I'd been honest until now, why change?

"Rockcliffe, yuppie central, no persons of colour or interest allowed." I replied. The pause that followed was awkward. I'd tried to be funny, but nobody was laughing. Or even smiling.

"Why's that?" Wispy asked.

"It's a made up rule, Irene." Ashleigh turned back to me. "You looking for trouble, bitch?" Her voice was a tense whisper, inviting a fight.

"Why? I have enough trouble: my dad lost his job, the bank took our house and our car because the lawyer took all our money, and now I can't go to university next year. Why would I want more trouble?"

"Maybe you're suicidal." Ashleigh said. There was a brief pause, and then everyone laughed.

"Miss too-good-for-you ain't any better than the rest of us now." She leaned in to me, "Are you?"

I shrugged, tacitly agreeing with her, but I knew better. This place was a dead end for them, but I still had plans, I was still going places. I wasn't a loser, like they were.

After a few seconds, Ashleigh nodded, and gestured for me to sit down. I'd always heard on cop shows and movies the term, "Stand Down." I knew what it was but I had never understood what that meant until now. One by one, her crew "stood down" and I was in. Well, I wasn't exactly out anymore, anyway.

14

A skinny blond, who was a combination of facial piercings, and the prim, sour looks of a librarian, pulled out another beer and opened it. She offered it to Ashleigh who instead offered it to me for a swig. I knew what my Dad would say but didn't care. These girls had just accepted me, the last thing I wanted to do was annoy them. And so I took a drink.

And saw the most amazing sight of my life.

I'm sure my jaw dropped and my eyes glazed over. I felt the beer fizz over my chin and onto my shirt. But I couldn't think about any of that, my brain just froze. His eyes were a dark liquid brown, broken only by bronze flecks. His hair was short and shiny, black with an oil-like sheen of blue in the sun. His skin was warmly tanned and looked soft and smooth as a baby's. I felt someone yank the beer from my hand, vague noises my brain interpreted as curses over the spilled beer drifted past my uncaring ears. I think I moaned.

He brushed past the girls and they let him go without a word spoken, I continued my mental checklist as he stepped forward; full kissable lips, thick eyelashes to die for, just an inch taller than me, perfection. Then, he paused to look me over. In that heartbeat, I felt him breathe. He just stood there, his dark eyes unreadable. After a full minute of staring at each other, he spoke, his voice soft with a lilting accent.

"Could you get out of the way, please? I need to go inside."

"I.. um… I'm sorry, I was just…" I felt stupider than I ever had in my whole life. I must've turned beet red.

"Excuse me?" He waited patiently.

As I stepped slightly to the left, he brushed past me without a second glance. He hadn't really noticed me, except as an obstacle to go around. How could I be so relieved and so disappointed at the same time?

The girls scornfully called rude words after him, but I hardly noticed. I was too busy dying of embarrassment. He hated me.

Then the librarian noticed me again. She called the attention of the others to my humiliation, laughing at my disappointment. I already felt like killing myself, she was offering me the knife for my wrists.

Then Ashleigh did something totally unexpected. She stood up for me.

"Yeah, like none of you dropped your drawers when he turned up last year? I never saw so many fucking cats in heat."

There was a moment of silence but Irene saved the day with a laugh, even if it was sheepish. "I never looked that stunned bunny, did I? I mean, the way she was drooling, it's a wonder Faraj didn't slip and break his neck."

Faraj, I thought. He was a Muslim, possibly Iraqi, or Lebanese. I'd seen a few in the past but they didn't look anything like him, at least, nowhere near that beautiful. For a brief instant, I started to envision what I would look like with a hijab on my head. But the fight that was brewing shook me from the dream.

The skinny blond had clearly said something bad to Ashleigh.

"You really think you're so cool, Francine?" Ashleigh spat, not letting words go unanswered. "You're the one that was acting like a whore over some fucking raghead in front of your own mother."

"I'm not the whore, bitch! I'll fucking cut you if you call me that again."

"Cut me with what?" She stuck her middle finger up. "Your bulimia finger?"

"Fuck you!"

A woman no one would mistake for a happy homemaker stuck her head out the second floor window and screamed, "What the hell is going on? I'll call the cops..." As she caught sight of us, she calmed down. "Oh, Ashleigh, it's you. You kids keep it down, the soaps are on." She pulled back in the window. I seemingly was the only one surprised by what just happened.

Ashleigh just shrugged. "That's my mother."

Great, we were neighbours.

Ashleigh

I was eager to see who'd be moving into Snake's old apartment. Of course, I couldn't let the others see; I'd look stupid, as eager as a little kid looking for someone new to play with. But the truth was, I was sick of my friends. Sick of this street, sick of being tough all the time, sick of being poor, sick of everything.

I was especially sick of Jeff, my mom's druggie boyfriend. It beat me how a smart woman like her always picked such losers. But this one was the worst.

At least with Snake's midnight move, his major drug connection was gone. It was too much to hope that he'd straighten up though. He'd probably already found another dealer.

I leaned casually against the moving truck, and lit my last smoke. I didn't even know what I was hoping for, something to get me out of my life, I guess. I didn't get it.

What a wimpy, prissy little daddy's girl that was, coming down the front steps like she owned the place. And look at the sour expression on her face, like she thinks it smells here. The others stirred restlessly, they didn't like her.

"You shouldn't be leaning on the truck, my dad won't like it." I couldn't believe she said that. Challenging me right in front of everyone. Was she suicidal? Maybe she was just stupid.

I pushed myself off the truck, blowing out a thin stream of smoke from the cigarette. I'd always thought that looked threatening when I saw it in the movies.

She cringed, I hadn't even done anything and she cringed. Good god, what was she doing moving here?

"Hi. We're just moving in."

The girls rolled their eyes while I just continued staring.

"No shit, Sherlock," I looked her up and down, her clothes said money. Those were Tommy Hilfiger jeans, and not from the Goodwill either. They were bought new. Her t-shirt was covered in glitter, who would wear that to schlep boxes unless they didn't own any old ragged ones?

I could almost hear Francine adding up how much this boob was worth. Francine thought of everything in terms of money, and hated people who had more than she did. And since she didn't have any...

Then I heard her dad coming down the stairs. I knew it was him, hard, fast and clicking steps. New shoes, lots of energy. There was no-one else it could be. I was pleased to still remember what my dad had taught me about tracking, I was only five when he went to jail.

I could find out more later, I didn't want to meet her dad, not like this. So I pushed myself off the truck and, flicking my cigarette butt at her, leaned in close, smelling perfumed soap.

"Watch your step, daddy's girl because if you make a wrong move, I'll cut your pretty face." Francine was quick to second that. She was always looking for a fight.

"She's done it before, even did time for assaulting some skank." Two months in foster care, with other native kids too young to go to jail, too bad to ignore. But it sounded serious when Francine said it.

After supper, I was just hanging on the porch with the gang. I'd lifted a couple of Jeff's beer, and Francine had them out of sight in her backpack. I hated the taste of it, but a few beers certainly softened the edges. Not as much as grass did, but Jeff would've noticed anything gone from his stash.

Soon enough, I heard the new girl's footsteps tripping lightly downstairs. Like she had the world on a silver plate, I wasn't sure if I hated or envied her, but I was definitely puzzled by her. Why was a rich kid moving into this neighbourhood?

I soon found out. They weren't rich anymore, though the snobby little bint still acted like she owned the world. I was curious to see what Francine would do. But I'd have to stop her if she went too far, last thing I needed was another brush with the cops. Even Jeff was better than that, I could avoid him.

Then that little shit, Muslim creep showed up. Always staring at my boobs or butt, and calling me a whore if I called him on it. How did a fifteen year old boy learn to act like that, anyway? Not from his uncle, he seemed a decent sort. Smelled like weird spices all the time, but that was to be expected. You don't eat all those amazing smelling curries without absorbing some of the spices.

Not like the prepackaged crap that was all her mom had time to make. Even birthdays were cake mixes and cans of frosting.

Could be worse, though. She could be Francine, and barf up her own birthday cake.

Faraj

I couldn't believe those stupid girls. Standing around the porch like they were the only ones who needed to use them. It was bad enough to see them smoking and drinking in public, like common whores, but then to force me to talk to them, by standing right in my way...

Wait a minute, who was the girl who'd been in my way? I didn't remember seeing her before. But it didn't matter, she was drinking beer. The Mullah had been very clear about such things.

Your body was sacred; you don't destroy it with alcohol or stimulants. And decent women were modest, and polite. They didn't curse and wear short tops, showing off their bellies, or pierce themselves to wear jewellery.

But it was a bit confusing, I couldn't stop myself from staring at them, it made me feel guilty, but the older boys said that was the girls' fault that I felt that way, not mine.

Opening my backpack, I pulled out the books I'd picked up at Fadi's. They were essays on true Islam, and the holy war on the West. My grandmother would be upset if she saw them, and my uncle would take me to the Mosque for another day-long lecture on compromise.

Why didn't they understand that I don't want to compromise? I don't want to be moderate and tolerant and make allowances for everything. I was angry and hurting and wanted someone to pay for it. I wanted to be strong like my mother. I don't even remember my father, so why did it matter what he'd believed.

But I remembered the day my mom died. I was only seven, but she'd explained everything, just as if I were already a man.

When I was just a baby, the Shi'tes in the south rebelled against Saddam Hussain. The U.S. had promised support and then bailed when the war started. Our people were rounded up, tortured and executed, thousands of them. Including my father. She never forgave the west for that.

She died fighting them.

I slid the books between my mattress and box spring. Fadi said he had a way to fix things. To make everything balance out. I just had to trust him. And read the books he'd lent me.

Samantha

Monday, just over a week before school. I had no idea where any of my school stuff was, and Mom had just thrown a fit and declared that half of the stuff in the house had to be thrown out or be given to charity. And, as usual when Mom got into these moods, she wanted it done *today*!! And since I had no idea what was in each box, that gave my Mom the excuse to randomly choose boxes and suggest that they either be thrown out or saved. I think she does it deliberately.

"You know you don't need fourteen boxes, Samantha. It's a small room, just throw out some of this…" She paused in the way mothers do when they are deciding what word would hurt best. "…crap." It worked.

""It's not crap, Mom! It's memories!" I tried not to yell but the tears were already starting to show. "Don't you get it? This is all I have now."

"And what about us?" she asked in that hurt way mothers use.

"What about you? You're the ones who got me into this." I thought for a second I'd gone too far as now Mom started to get mad. She didn't want to live like this either but unlike me; she reined herself in, and continued in a frighteningly calm and patient voice.

"I don't care how you do it, open them up and search through them, or just arbitrarily throw them out, but I want at least ten boxes piled by the front door by supper." Then she was gone.

"This is so unfair!" I yelled back as she disappeared. But I was getting used to unfair. I looked around and then made a quick calculation. There were fourteen boxes and only seven hours until supper. If I didn't stop for lunch, I'd have a half an hour per box. Not nearly enough time but at least it was something.

I slammed the door shut making sure the whole building heard me, but there wasn't any reaction from Mom. As far as she was concerned, she had laid down the law and I just had to obey.

I started pulling boxes onto my bed, one at a time, to go through them. The first held my old yearbooks, report cards and certificates from Montessori Academy. I'd received awards for my English and French marks three years running. I had to keep those; they were special. Okay, they proved I was special. And my yearbooks were my only link to my real friends, I ignored that small voice that said I'd given them my new phone number and none of them had called me back. After all, it had only been a few days, and school starts next week. They're probably busy.

"One box down and nothing thrown out," I thought. This was going to be harder than I thought.

The next box had my old stuffed toys from when I was baby. I smiled as I pulled out my favourite, an old blue Grumpy Bear, a frown permanently stitched to his face. I totally agreed with his mood, so he went onto my pillow. My Princess Barbie collection was probably worth money now; it had to stay. A popular baby doll that cried when laid on her back. She was definitely my favourite back then. *Back then.* I stopped and looked in the box realizing that at some point in my life, everything in this box was a favourite. Why would I have kept them if they weren't? Box number two found its way into my closet.

Box three: books. The smell of the paper was instantly thrilling. These books were what kept me alive. The Ghost of Colby Drive, definitely a keeper, it gave me the chills every time I read it. And it's sequel, The Curse of the Moonless Knight. The Cecil Castellucci series alone kept me from going insane from mom's stupid rules. She had a way of making you see the humour in the most frustrating parts of being a teen. Especially in Boy Proof. But now, all read and mostly abused, they were no longer a part of me. Besides, unlike my yearbooks or dolls, these could be donated. Maybe some kid in a school or hospital might find a friend in them the same way I did.

I dumped the box on the floor just outside my room making sure Mom heard it. I added a loud, "One!" to make the point perfectly clear.

"I said ten!" was all I heard back. Bitch.

Winter clothes greeted me in box four. This was an easy keeper. Or so I thought as boxes five and six were also packed to the brim with down, fleece and wool clothes meant for the harsh winters of Canada. They had to be kept. But the math said otherwise. I was already at six boxes kept and I had only eight more to go. Then it hit me. Mom said she wanted ten boxes piled by the door by suppertime. She never said they had to be full. Maybe she just wanted the cardboard boxes gone. I could have easily found out by a king but figured that if I was wrong, then I'd be back where I started. Better to err on the side of clutter, I thought.

By lunch I was starting to worry. My room was fuller than I'd ever seen, and I still had more boxes to look through. There was just no way that I could do what she wanted, even if I threw out ten empty boxes. No matter how I looked at my room, nothing was going to change what I'd been dreading all along. We were here to stay and the life I had was gone.

I threw the half empty box at the wall, raining jewellery and souvenirs onto the ratty carpet. God, I hated this place! I hated my parents for doing this to me. I wanted everything back the way it was, and if I couldn't have that, I didn't want anything.

I knew I sounded like a spoilt brat, and hated myself for it, but not enough to behave differently. Maybe this was the universe's way of telling me to wake up and smell the coffee. I hated coffee.

Ashleigh

I snuck in the house as quietly as possible. Mom was on late shift, she'd left by four. That meant Jeff and I were alone.

I turned the key silently; I kept it rubbed with Vaseline just for this. My room was just past the living room, maybe twenty feet away. If I was quiet enough, or lucky enough, Jeff would be out looking to score, and I'd be safe behind a locked door in a few seconds.

I wasn't that lucky.

"Hey little girl, where you been?" His voice was slurred, stoned. A cold chill worked its way up my scalp.

I tried to slide back out the door, but he was there, pushing it closed behind me. How could he move so quietly while that drunk or stoned? He must've known I was coming home now, hidden in the closet.

But I had to think of how to get out of there. He was dangerous when we were alone.

I took a step toward the hall to my bedroom but he grabbed my arm, pulling me closer. I could smell stale beer on his breath. He leaned in, groping for my shirt, and I automatically pulled back. My shirt ripped, and the sight of my bra seemed to surprise him.

Taking advantage of his momentary stunned look, I kicked his ankle and broke free. I didn't count on his wearing his work boots in the house though. The kick just glanced off and barely slowed him down. He caught me outside my bedroom. I wish I'd been a tle faster, the lock I'd put on inside my room was supposed to be impossible to break.

I tried to knee him, but he was expecting it, my knee just bounced off his thigh. He yelled something and punched me in the face. I was so shocked, I stopped fighting. He grabbed my breast and that woke me up again, this time my knee went straight to his nards. He whimpered and sank down, letting go of me. I ran down the hall.

I dodged right and made it to the bathroom and locked the door. But the stupid lock was made to open from the outside. A safety feature, the landlord called it when we moved in. Yeah, I feel real safe right now. The window was small, but I was pretty skinny. The downside was, if he busted through the door while I was halfway out, or stuck....

My ass would be in his face, and there would be nothing I could do about it.

Samantha

There was a sudden knocking on the front door; Mom was so startled that she dropped the box she was carrying. After a second, I got up to answer the door. Mom hopped up to stop me, but then paused. She looked torn, scared but feeling foolish about it, I guess.

"Wait, Samantha. Look through the peephole first. This isn't as safe a neighbourhood as Rockcliffe."

"I know, Mom. I'm not three." But I had forgotten. I felt stupid for just rushing to the door like a kid. Then I looked through the peephole and saw it was Ashleigh, and felt stupid for being paranoid. So, I looked at Mom as if it was her fault that I was being stupid.

"It's just Ashleigh from downstairs. Honestly, you're so freaking paranoid."

I opened the door and noticed that Ashleigh was looking back down the hall toward the stairs. When she heard my door open, she came in really fast, without waiting for me to invite her.

I started to say something, and then noticed that her eye was going all purple and her lip was bleeding a little. It looked like she'd been in a fight.

"Holy shit! What happened to you?"

My mom acted prissy and objected to my language. Then she got a look at Ashleigh's face.

"I'm calling the police. And an ambulance."

Ashleigh looked panicky, "No! I'm fine; it was just a stupid fight. "

Mom looked reluctant to leave it alone, but Ashleigh looked more afraid of the cops than of whomever she'd fought with.

"Well, I suppose. If you're sure you're okay"

"I'm fine Mrs. H; I've had far worse before."

Mom didn't look reassured at that, but Ashleigh hustled me out of the room before she could raise any more objections.

We were both sitting on my bed; my desk chair was piled high with unsorted stuff. Ashleigh looked around; more as if she was avoiding my eye than as if she was interested in my crap. I waited impatiently. I felt that I had to do something, but I didn't want to sound like my mom. I wanted her to ask for my help. She didn't. After awhile, she just stopped looking around and stared at her feet. This was so unlike the pushy Ashleigh I'd seen so far, it scared me more than the bruises did.

"Who hit you? Was it Francine?" I couldn't help blurting out questions; I was too scared for her. And for me, if there was someone getting Ashleigh this afraid, I needed to know who it was, so that I would know to steer clear of them myself. There was so much I didn't know about this place.

She just shook her head and whispered something I didn't catch. Then she got up to close my door.

"It was my mom's boyfriend." I was flabbergasted.

"Why?" I almost said what did you do, but changed it at the last second to a question less likely to get me my own set of bruises.

"He's an asshole. I can't wait until she dumps him."

"But why did he hit you? What did you do?" Oops.

"I didn't do fucking nothing!" I must've cringed a bit, because she looked sorry, and leaned forward to whisper again. "It was because I wouldn't do any fucking nothing, you know?" She waited, one eyebrow arched over a blackening eye.

I shook my head, she couldn't mean what I thought she meant. No way.

"I won the fight, though. I punched him right in the nards. They practically came out his nose." She laughed at this, but I was horrified.

"Did you tell your mom?"

"Why, you think she'll dump him because I say so? He'll just say I'm lying. I just have to try not to be there when Mom's at work."

"Did you try telling her? Maybe she'll call the cops on him."

Ashleigh just snorted, but I could see the idea appealed to her.

"You know what they do to paedophiles in jail?" She smiled for the first time since arriving. I felt this was a good moment to ask a question that had been bothering me.

"Why did you come here?" I asked.

I thought I would have to explain more but I could see Ashleigh knew where I was going. She looked around at the room and all the clutter. She went straight for my crying doll. I figured she would rather check out my stuff than answer my question. It figured, really. She was here to hide out, not to be my friend.

Picking up the doll, Ashleigh knew exactly what to do. She laid the doll on its back and it cried on cue…so did Ashleigh, and just a quietly. This shocked me but it was nothing compared to the shock that was to come. With the third cry, Ashleigh curled up and sobbed. She looked eight or nine and more innocent than me.

"Do you have one of those?" I asked.

She nodded as she turned to me. Then her expression flattened and her tears stopped, "Had."

"You moved and had to throw it out?"

"No. I…" There was a memory that she wasn't ready to share. "I lost it."

"Was it your favourite doll?"

"It was my only doll."

The room seemed to spin a little as I looked around at what I had believed to be treasures. In a single moment, they all turned to junk in my eyes. I suddenly wanted to throw everything out and just start over again. Find new memories; find new things to put in my room make it mine. And although I had gotten rid of a few things, there was one that I knew had to go.

"You want to keep her?" Ashleigh looked at me, not sure what to say. I continued, "Seriously, you take her." I wouldn't say there were tears in her eyes but Ashleigh's face showed something that probably hadn't been there in years. She was touched. Wordlessly, she nodded and held the doll tight.

"She's yours then," I said.

The silence continued for a few moments, and then Ashleigh glared at me. "This doesn't mean I like you."

I nodded, believe me, I could tell what she'd thought when she'd come in. Her look at our leather furniture was both envious and disgusted.

My Mom yelled up that she wasn't hearing much unpacking going on. I rolled my eyes and asked Ashleigh if she's like to help me get rid of some of my things. She agreed on the condition that if she saw something she liked, she could keep it. We had a deal and by supper time, eight boxes were ready for the curb, and two were going home with Ashleigh. And, Ashleigh decided to stay for supper. I acted like it was my idea. Four years of drama school was going to come in handy here.

For the first time since we moved, I felt like things might be looking up.

CHAPTER TWO

Life starts

Samantha

For the last eleven years, school started in September, the day after Labour Day. Starting in August seemed like such a cruel thing to do. Yet here I was, knowing that I had to get up at seven for the first time in two months. I should have been sleeping but my ears were filled with Ashleigh's mother and her boyfriend's voices. They'd been drinking, I could tell. They didn't always make sense, but you couldn't stop listening. The wall was like cardboard for one thing; it was like they were right in the room with me. Worse, the wall seemed to act like the skin of a drum, amplifying their shouts as if each of them was using a megaphone.

"Ball-busting bitch! I told you never to touch my stash, what the hell you thinking your doing, touching my stash? I told you!"

"Screw yourself, asshole, it's my house!"

I tried to ignore them; I rolled over trying to shove my pillow into my ear, but I could still hear everything. They were arguing over drugs, and occasionally over money. Once they segued into arguing over Ashleigh, but only long enough to recognize her name. Then it was back to drugs and money.

I couldn't believe the swearing they did. If my mom ever screamed curses like a sailor on leave, I'd die of shock. But enough was enough already, if either one of them swore again, I was going to start screaming myself.

Then my parents started. Great, I thought, fights in stereo. The language was different but the meaning was still the same. Everyone was angry at everyone else and someone had to get the blame. I was just thankful it wasn't me.

"David, don't you dare go over there, come back here."

"I'm not putting up with this, Margaret. I need to get some sleep."

"Why? It's not like you do anything all day."

"I am doing my best, we're not starving."

"Not starving? You think that's all that that matters? You think this is a fit neighbourhood for Samantha? You think I want to live like that?"

I could just picture her pointing toward Ashleigh's apartment. My Mom loved to point to get her message across.

"You think I do? I don't see you getting off your fat ass to look for work."

"What? How dare you talk to me like that?"

The door to Ashleigh's apartment slammed shut and I could hear someone walking away. I figured that would be the end to that argument.

"You think I agreed to marry you for this?" My Mom was on a roll and wasn't about to stop. "You promised me a good life, a damn good life and this is what you've given me! Let me ask you, David. Does this look like a good life?"

"This wasn't my fault!" my Dad screamed.

"*Everything* is your fault; you said you knew what you were
doing. I trusted you!" my Mom screamed back, twice as loud as
my Dad. It must have echoed through the building because
Ashleigh's mother pounded on the wall.

"You shut up in there! It's three AM! Don't you know this is a
school night? Decent people are trying to sleep."

I had to smother myself with the pillow to stop from groaning
out loud.

Mom and Dad whispered tensely for a little while and then an
even tenser silence fell. You could almost feel the chill spread
from their room, through the wall, into my room. The silence had a
presence all its own, like a dark ghost creeping stealthily into your
room. I actually preferred the yelling. It didn't sound as final as
the silence did.

I still got a few hours sleep.

In the morning, Mom was bitchy as hell. She didn't say much
other than a few muttered words under her breath. Dad was worse;
he grabbed a silent coffee and walked out. When I came into the
kitchen, Mom decided she too, wanted to be alone and I was left to
fend for myself. I guess they forgot that it was a school day. The
kitchen was still a mess. Most of the dishes were still in boxes and
I had to go searching for a bowl and spoon. All Mom had
unpacked was whatever we'd needed to use right then. She was
never much of a cooking person, despite buying every gadget
known to mankind.

The only cereal I could find was Dad's high fibre stuff, but at least it was food. Besides, if I was going to learn to be an adult, I figured I might as well learn what it's like to eat tasteless food for the sake of living a few extra years as an invalid.

I was so tired I thought I was going to fall asleep and drown in my cereal. Mom finally returned and saw just how out-of-it I was. She insisted that I drink some coffee. More adult behaviour, I thought. But even the bitter taste of the coffee couldn't fully awaken me. I just sat and stared like a zombie at my cereal bowl. Mom chirped about having to make my lunch because we didn't know if there was a cafeteria at the school. I guess she remembered about school after all. I asked her if maybe it would be best if I just went hungry and had a good dinner tonight but she insisted that I have a good lunch to keep up my strength. I figured that not arguing at three in the morning would have been better, but I kept my mouth shut.

Mom's make-up wasn't the most fashionable these days, but it did help to conceal some of the black under my eyes and the white pastiness of my skin. So, I put on a little concealer stuff under my eyes and a bit of blush for some colour on my face. Mom kept trying to pretend nothing was wrong, but she just seemed so fake. And brittle, like she was made of that crackled glass that was so popular a couple of years ago.

Finally Ashleigh knocked on the door. I was never so glad to go to school in my life.

Ashleigh

Seven o'clock in the freaking morning. Whose idea was it to have a seven in the morning, anyway? Some sadistic government clerk probably.

My eyes felt like sandpaper, and my hair was plastered to my neck with sweat. Mom and Jeff had argued half the night, and now they were both sleeping in, while I had to get up for school. I was tempted to say to hell with it and go back to sleep. But welfare was never going to pay enough to get away from here, so I had to find a job. And unless I wanted to say "you want fries with that?" for the rest of my life, that meant graduating.

I'd hoped when I heard the argument that mom might throw Jeff out, but no such luck. I'd heard him come in again at about five, so I was extra careful to be quiet.

As usual, there was no real food in the fridge. I managed a piece of toast and peanut butter, and decided to look for some cash to buy lunch at school. Mom had left her purse out, but Jeff had beaten me to it. The wallet was totally empty.

I wondered if Miss Priss upstairs had any money.

I grabbed a couple of cigarettes out of mom's jacket and headed upstairs.

Samantha

The Mary, Queen of Heaven High School stood before me. My imagination had painted a Victorian brick building with white pillars and marble floors. Reality was somewhat less impressive. Square cement block, windows that don't open, paved yard, no fields, no trees, and no benches. It looked as ugly and unfriendly as any building I'd ever seen. Ashleigh just headed on in like it was normal to enter such a dead and hopeless looking place.

A few of her usual crowd were hanging out on the steps, smoking. A weary, beaten-down looking teacher watched but didn't say anything.

I waved half-heartedly at Irene, and she waved back. The others in her group just peered at me suspiciously, but I was too cranky to give a shit.

The interior of the school failed to live up to the promise of the exterior, and that's saying something. I followed the signs to the office and dug through my backpack for my transfer papers.

I needn't have bothered. A bored looking secretary just dropped them into her inbox and asked what grade I was in. Then she typed my name into her computer and it spat out two forms; a class schedule and a book list. She dug out a pamphlet entitled *This is Your School, Too* and handed it to me with the other papers.

"If you want to add or drop classes, you have to do it by Friday. Missed classes count against your record, so make up your mind fast." Then she went back to what she'd been doing. Just like that, I was registered and dismissed.

Out in the hall, I glanced at my schedule. Holy crap! I was registered for every grade twelve class they had. Four of them this period alone! I glanced further down the page; I had at least two classes every period, and no lunch breaks. And the classes I missed would count? I sat down on the steps to look the schedule over carefully; I had to decide right away what I wanted to take.

It was better than I'd thought at first glance. Despite my schedule looking like there were a thousand choices, most of them were the same four classes, just at different times. Remedial Math, academic math and advanced math were each listed three times a week. I assumed that you were supposed to take it three times a week, so I crossed out all of the remedial and advanced ones. That was a start, anyway. The same was true of English, so I crossed out everything but the advanced classes. Same for French. It was starting to look better.

Then my papers went flying as someone crashed into me from behind. I was nearly flung off the step from the force.

"Forgive me; I didn't see you crouching there." The voice was familiar, and I hoped I was wrong. But it was Faraj, the gorgeous guy from the second floor. He stared at me for a moment before recognizing me. I probably looked just the same, blushing, embarrassed, and slack jawed.

Then he just sighed, like I was some kind of tribulation he was forced to endure. Not the most flattering feeling.

"Do you get in my way on purpose?"

"No, it's just a coincidence. Maybe you're in my way; you just think I'm in yours." Did that even make sense? I hated trying to sound smart and witty, it was too much pressure.

"Do you mind moving? I have a class to get to."

"Oh, I'm sorry." I stammered. I tried hard to pull myself together, I could be cool, I could be sophisticated, I was from Rockcliffe.

"So, you're on the second floor of my building. My name's Sam." I sounded like an idiot.

He looked down his elegant nose at me. "A decent woman doesn't talk to men she doesn't know." He looked me over and sounded kind of sad, like he hated pointing this out, "Only a whore flirts."

Well! He might be cute, but that was just plain rude. I reined my temper in sharply, it wouldn't do to be caught fighting in the halls on my first day.

"A decent man understands the difference between being friendly to his neighbours, and acting like a whore." He blinked at me a couple of times; you could almost see him switching tracks.

But I was too insulted to care about his sudden epiphany. I stalked off; head high in what I hoped was a dignified and suitably sexy but ladylike manner.

I forgot all my papers. Shit, I'd have to go back later and hope they were still there. I stalked around the corner, and then turned around to spy on him. As soon as he left, I'd run back for those blasted transfer papers. There was just no way I was turning around where he could see me, not after that exit.

Faraj

"A decent man understands the difference between being friendly to his neighbours, and acting like a whore."

She seemed angered by my comment, and here I was trying to help her see what she was doing wrong. Since she'd only just started hanging out with those loose women, she might still be saved. I was trying to help her!

I looked her over, realizing that she was dressed modestly, or at least with what passed for modesty in this sinful culture. And she was carrying a full load of books; maybe she wasn't the same as her friends.

But she turned on her heel and stalked off before I could apologize for offending her. I saw that she'd left her papers behind, so I gathered them up for her. They were her class schedule and registration forms. I couldn't resist peeking at them. She had just moved here from Rockcliffe. That was a much different neighbourhood, full of greedy and shameless men. Perhaps it was too late for her after all; she must be ruined by her upbringing. Then again, she was choosing almost all of the advanced classes on her schedule. And she was pretty, in a cleaner way than the others. She wore a little makeup, but it was restrained, not whorish.

And she was very pretty.

But Fadi had a lot to say about women, not much of it good. Especially North American women, who flaunted their bodies, then scorned the men they made lust after them. The prettier they were, the more cursed the man who wanted them. They were evil, a test to be passed only by avoiding and scorning them. They led men only to humiliation and death.

But Samantha seemed shy, and a bit lost. When she wasn't yelling at him, that is. Was it still a forbidden lust if he helped her find Allah, and she became a good woman, like the ones in his mother's country? If she became modest and proper, covered her flesh like she was supposed to...

I shook those thoughts out of my head, remembering I still had a handful of papers that weren't mine. Best to turn them in at the office, she would surely go there to ask for the lost and found.

Samantha

I couldn't believe it. He'd stolen all my papers. How was I supposed to finish registration if he took off with all my.... Oh no, I realized that I could be losing marks big time if I couldn't get those papers replaced.

I had pretty much figured out what classes I wanted and so headed back to the office to see if I could register without the forms. I was starting to panic, what if they insisted I hand in the originals? Why did that rude, smug, little jerk have to steal my papers? Just being mean, I decided.

I went to the front desk and the same bored receptionist. She didn't even look at me. She just pointed at the same pile as my transfer had gone into.

"Excuse me; I need you to register me right away." She finally looked up.

"Why?"

"Why? I need my schedule; I can't afford to miss classes. I need to keep my marks up if I'm going to get a scholarship to university."

"What makes you think you'll get a scholarship?" She actually snorted at me!

I proudly raised my chin and said in my best 'I'm way too good for you' voice; "Well, I'm already on the McGill University early acceptance list. All I have to do is keep my GPA above 3.9. And it's 3.97 now, assuming this school doesn't totally ruin it."

She gaped at me for a second then dug for my transcript in the untidy pile in her inbox. Papers scattered everywhere without her seeming to notice.

I started to tell her I'd lost it, but then she found it, I guess Faraj had turned it in. I felt kind of sorry for bad-mouthing him, even if he didn't know what I'd been thinking. Just as well, I didn't think that losing my papers would've proved my point about being too smart for this school.

The receptionist called the principal out of his office. I was starting to think that my mouth had finally gotten me into trouble, but I really needed someone to realize that I was special. I didn't belong here, I was too intelligent, too classy, too… everything.

They gave me my schedule and a late pass and sent me to Civics class. I could hear them whispering and was dying to know what they were saying, but I had to get to Civics.

I was really happy to see both Faraj and Ash were in my class. Though I was a bit worried about his figuring out what I'd been thinking. I wouldn't tell him, of course, but I'd say thanks later for taking my stuff to the office. I carefully chose a chair in front of him, so that he wasn't in my line of sight.

The teacher was grossly fat, but seemed nice enough. I just wished she didn't have such a little girl voice. It grated on my ears. It was like having Lisa Simpson teach the class.

The afternoon was just like most hot, hazy afternoons in Ottawa. Air quality alerts, smog warnings, and a feeling like there was no oxygen at ground level. Except that instead of trying to avoid the

heat in a nice, air-conditioned home, I was dealing with a
combination of stuffy air and even stuffier teachers. They all
seemed to play by the same rulebook. Make the least amount of
effort possible, look really put out if someone asked a question, and
make it seem as if it were our fault we got nothing out of it. If they
had even seen what teachers were like at Montessori, they would
have put away their chalk and died of embarrassment. I breezed
through the classes with only one concern. Ash wasn't in math
class. Not even a day in and she was already skipping classes. I
forgot that she might be in remedial.

As school ended, the weather went from bad to worse. The wind
picked up and then, just as I was about to leave the building, it
rained. Poured! I thought about waiting for the storm to pass but
after 10 minutes, it seemed as if this wasn't just passing through. I
was getting up the nerve to start walking home, when Ash came
around the corner of the building. She was soaked to the skin, and
weaving a little. So were the two girls with her. She peered up at
me through her dripping bangs, then pointed me out to her friends
and laughed. I figured this wasn't going to be the friendly Ash.

"Look, it's the little lost sheep." She wove her way to me, and
stared up at me, clearly puzzled.

"What're you doing, white girl? You forget the way home?" I
just noticed then that her two friends were Native, like her. I was
worried for a moment, but they seemed amused, not angry, about
Ash talking to me. Ash drew up close enough for me to smell the
alcohol on her breath. My heart sank.

"Onhka thi?" One of her friends bleared at me, who's that?

"Ontiatshi ne ki." Ashleigh replied in the same language, this is my friend.

"Tanon' onhka ne: nakaonha? Who is she?"

"kara:ken – white girl." They all laughed, and I shrugged, like I didn't care that they talked about me like I wasn't even there.

"So, you just gonna stand there?" Ash asked.

"I was hoping it would stop raining. I didn't bring an umbrella this morning."

"You made out of white sugar? You afraid you're gonna melt?" They all laughed at that, but it wasn't a mean laugh, so I joined in.

Ash slung her arm around my shoulder and hauled me off the steps into the monsoon. Within seconds my hair was plastered into my eyes, except for the parts that instantly frizzed up like a poodle on speed. One of the other girls stared at me, her eyes going wide.

"Wow, I wish I had curly hair." I was floored. Her hair was a thick black mass, cascading down her back like night. I'd have sold my eye teeth for her hair.

We started off down the street, Ash practically pulling me along. I wanted to ask her about missing class that afternoon, but just couldn't seem to fit it into the weird, wandering, surreal conversation the three were having. They acted like they'd forgotten I was even there, though Ash kept her arm crooked around my neck. I didn't mind, it was the only part of me that was still dry.

Mom was looking out the window, waiting for me, when I got home. The other girls continued on down the street and Ash and I went into the building. I heard our door open while Ash fumbled with her apartment keys. Then she realized that the door was unlocked already, and seemed to sober up instantly.

"Hey, white girl, you think I could stay with you tonight? You know, like girl's night or something? Just until two, when my mom gets home?"

"Samantha, what are you doing down there?" My mom did not sound happy, so I shook my head at Ash.

"Tonight's probably not good. My mom hates me doing anything on a school night, and I couldn't call to tell her I'd be late because my cell phone got shut off, she'll be really pissed at me. Maybe on the weekend?"

"Weekend's no point. My mom only works during the week. It's when we're alone that Jeff's dangerous."

"Samantha Lea Hunter, get up here," My Mom roared. Ash glanced at the ceiling and nodded sadly. I looked to her but all she did was slowly slip into her apartment, silent as a ghost.

I started up the stairs. "We all have our cross to bear," Grammy used to say. Mine was fuming at the top of the stairs but I was more worried about Ash's.

Supper was a tense, cold-shouldered event. Mom wasn't speaking to me. She took my excuse about not having a cell phone anymore as a personal criticism, and I felt like a moron when she asked if the school had pay phones, so I lied and said no. Dad was mad at Mom for throwing out the stuff he said she could throw out yesterday. I guess he changed his mind after he started organizing his desk. And I was mad at both of them because while they were complaining about the most irrelevant stuff in the world, Ash was alone with a monster.

After supper, Mom decided that I was going to do the dishes while she got a bit of air. It had stopped raining, but the air was still so heavy and wet that you could hardly breathe. As soon as I heard the front door close, I phoned Ash's place. There was no answer.

I washed the dishes in a frenzy, not bothering to dry them, and then scurried downstairs. I paused to listen outside Ash's door and heard nothing. No TV, no radio. I pulled in a deep breath and held it. Then I knocked, quietly at first, then louder. Nothing.

Then I heard crying out back, by the dumpster.

I peered out and saw Ash, with her head on her knees, her shirt ripped. She looked up when I opened the door, fear in her eyes.

"Oh my God, Ash. What happened?"

"Leave me alone, white girl." She just turned her face away, looking so hurt and alone that my chest hurt looking at her.

"Ash?" I couldn't think of a thing to say. Nothing I thought of seemed to be worth saying. But it didn't matter, she just ignored me. So, I went back in to look for my mom. She'd know what to do.

Mom was on the porch talking an older woman in loose, foreign looking clothing. It was brightly coloured, with embroidered hems. She wore a scarf that covered all of her hair and tucked up under her chin, not quite a hijab, but not just a scarf either... Mom looked interested in what she was saying, the anger she's been radiating since we'd moved wasn't there anymore.

Then I noticed that Faraj was sitting a few steps down from the women. Ash went right out of my mind; forgotten like I had never seen her.

Faraj was dressed in a jacket and tie; he looked so gorgeous I didn't notice how angry he was for a few seconds. You could almost hear his teeth grind together.

I stepped down to the stair just above him, and he turned to stare at me.

"You look like a drowned rat." Well, it wasn't the most romantic start to a conversation, but he did notice my hair.

"I got caught in the rain." He nodded toward the stair by his side, so I sat down, heart pounding.

"Did you see the news tonight?" He asked as if this was a test, or a challenge. I was going to lose because I never watch the news. I shook my head not even offering an excuse.

"Someone just tried to blow up a train station in London." His voice was odd, flat. Like he was being careful not to show what he felt.

"Why would they bother with London's train station? Toronto is so much bigger. And Ottawa's far more important, it's the capital." He looked at me as if I were speaking gibberish.

"London, England." He corrected me. "They're claiming it was an unprovoked attack by Muslim extremists. They aren't even looking at anyone else."

The old woman said something sharp in another language, and Faraj replied in the same tongue. She shook her head and he jumped up and down to the bottom of the steps.

"I'm sorry, I have to leave now. I'm meeting my uncle." His voice was polite, but kind of flat, like that wasn't what he'd wanted to say at all. He strode away, back straight.

I wondered what that was about; it was obviously about more than the bombing. But trust grownups to think we couldn't handle anything negative or scary. They thought we needed to be protected from the news, as if we didn't know what the world was like. As if we were little princesses in a fairy tale fussing over a pea in our bed, when things were happening in our own lives like what going on with Ashleigh…. Oh my God, I had forgotten Ash completely.

Ashleigh

"Stupid white bitch." She just walked away, like she couldn't see something was wrong. Little princess probably couldn't see past her own blond perfect nose. Do I look okay? Do I look like there's nothing wrong? No! But off she went, happy as a freaking lark. To hell with her.

I just sat there, wondering what to do. I didn't dare stay here, it was too close to the apartment, but I didn't know where else to go. I had been hoping to go up to white girl's place; Jeff would never bother me there. But white girl was too full of herself to notice I'm upset. And scared, I had to admit, Jeff had never been really violent before, just pushy.

I decided to go find Carrie Whitehorse. A little something to get a buzz on, dull the pain. That's what I needed, and Carrie always had good stuff. For a moment I wondered how to pay for it, but figured Carrie'd be okay with fronting me the stuff. She knew I was good for it, and this was an emergency.

I pulled myself to my feet; I couldn't believe how much I hurt. It felt like Jeff had cracked a couple of my ribs, maybe my arm, too. I gritted my teeth to keep from crying, I absolutely was not going to cry over this bastard. I was Mohawk, the greatest race of warriors on Earth and I was not going to cry.

A tear slipped out anyway.

This time it was beyond just creepy, it was really scary. What if I didn't get away next time? What if he managed to... really hurt me? My mind skittered along the edges of what he was trying to do, I usually joked about it, but I was terrified of him.

What if he killed me to prevent my calling the cops? What if he killed my mom too?

Then white girl came back.

Faraj

I could feel the hairs on the back of my neck bristle with anger. I imagined you could practically see sparks, like my hair was made of small electrical wires. I knew how rude I must look, stomping off in anger, and I was sorry to disappoint Fadi. I knew he wanted me to stay polite, fit in, and do nothing to draw attention. But I was so angry at my grandmother. At everything and everybody.

Those men in London, who'd tried to strike a blow against the non-believers, were only a little older than me. I couldn't imagine what it took to drive to the place where you knew you were going to die. To sacrifice everything for what you believed in. I was stunned by the thought, unable to wrap my brain around that kind of courage. Or foolhardiness. I wasn't sure I agreed with their actions, I mean, I understood their anger. That was for sure, but to kill innocent people? Soldiers, yes. They knew they could be killed when they signed up. They might even deserve it. But children? Pregnant women? Students?

I felt so confused. I had to talk to Fadi; he'd be able to explain things so they made sense again.

Although I didn't like Fadi's friend Ali, I had to respect him as a brother. He had learned Allah's will as a child, his father was a Mullah. Which he never let me forget, and never stopped pointing out that my grandmother and uncle were liberals. Trying to fit in. They were to be hated, as I was supposed to hate the people who lived here.

But they weren't all bad. And I loved my grandmother. I didn't agree with her politics, but I loved her.

Samantha

I couldn't believe my mother! How dare she just brush me off like a five year old? Neither she nor Faraj's grandmother wanted to hear anything I was saying about Ash. They'd rather keep talking about whatever stupid thing they were on about, than hear about some real problems. Well, screw them; I could look after it myself. Jeff wouldn't dare touch me.

I stomped back through the downstairs hallway to the rear door. I hoped Ash was still there. She had to call the police, rape was a serious crime. Jeff would be put in jail for a long time. Long enough for Ash to get away from here, anyway. I ignored the little voice that asked where she could go, university? Medical school?

Ash was standing near the edge of the dumpster, well, almost standing. She was hunched over, like her ribs hurt. Somehow she looked worse standing there, bravely trying to look like there was nothing wrong, than she had all curled up and crying.

I walked over slowly. I was scared, how could I fix this? I'm fifteen years old, who am I kidding? I needed to get my mom. But just then Ash looked up with such pain and hope in her face. I couldn't walk away again, not even to grab my mom.

CHAPTER THREE

Things get deeper

Ashleigh

She was back! She didn't just walk away. But she was alone; she didn't bring her mom, or even one of the gang. I wondered why not.

She hurried over, then stood there, doing nothing. Just dragging her toes through the dirt, like a two year old caught doing something wrong. She didn't even look at me.

Finally she glanced up.

"What do you want to do?"

I wanted to run away, I wanted to kill Jeff, I wanted to kill my mother for taking his side and refusing to believe me, I wanted to kill myself.

"Let's get high," I said. "Do you have any money?"

"No. but I think I know where my dad has some." She shrugged, looking unhappy. "What good does getting stoned do? It won't stop anything."

But she turned and went back into the building anyway. So I followed her. I gasped, hoping that the pain in my ribs was only a bruise.

We went upstairs as quietly as we could, hearing her mother talking on the porch.

"My dad's supposed to be looking for work. He usually just goes out to Starbucks and reads the paper, though. He says it makes him feel like everything's back the way it should be."

I snorted. Starbucks, home of the five buck coffee. You could get a couple of beer for that, if you had someone to buy it for you. "Stay by the door and listen for my mom, I'll go see if he has a twenty in his stash." So, they kept money in the apartment, good to know. It might be necessary to steal some sometime. I watched carefully to see where she went, but at the last moment, she turned waving at me to go back to the door. At least I knew it was down the hall, toward the bedrooms.

Samantha

I didn't feel right about this, stealing money from my parents. But Ash looked devastated, and I had to admit, the thought of doing drugs was kind of exciting. I'd never done anything really bad before, I'd always been conscious of how it would affect my getting into med school, but what was the point now?

It wasn't like I really had a future anymore, not like I did last year, before dad screwed up and lost everything. So what difference did it make if I stole a little money? They didn't give me any for school anymore, so they kind of owed it to me.

So why was my heart pounding so hard I couldn't hear the radio in the kitchen playing? My head felt light and kind of tingly with nerves. I was such a freaking wuss.

So, I ignored the small voice that said this was very wrong, and opened my parent's bedroom door. I knew Dad kept his emergency money in an envelope in his underwear drawer; he'd done that since I was a baby.

There it was, just like I figured. He had about seventy bucks, so I slipped thirty out of the envelope. For a minute I considered putting ten back, but decided it wouldn't make any difference. Either he knew how much he had or he didn't. I realized that this was one of those turning points the history teacher mentioned. I could still put the money back. No-one would know.

Then I thought of Ash's face. And my shattered dream of being a famous surgeon. So, I slipped the money into my back pocket and closed the drawer.

Ashleigh

I jiggled up and down on my toes; my grandfather would've said I had ants in my pants. I grimaced, the thought of anything in my pants right now made me feel sick.

What was taking white girl so long; she said she knew where the money was. I wondered if she'd been lying to me.

What would Mrs. Hunter do if she came up and found me here? What if white girl took the money and went out the back door? Money missing and a native hanging out alone in the apartment meant only one thing. I'd be joining my dad in jail. Well, not quite, I knew they didn't put teenage girls in the men's prison… but that just reminded me of what Jeff was after again.

I felt cold and anxious, and wanted to get to Carrie's for the grass. That would calm me down, and then maybe I could think of how to survive until mom got sick of Jeff's lying and stealing.

All I probably needed was another month or two. They were starting to fight all the time, so she'd throw him out soon. I just wished she'd believed me when I started to tell her what he was up to. But she was hurting for her fix and he always had stuff. So she sided with him. My fault. I should've thought to wait until after she was high.

What the hell was taking so long? Did she want her mother to catch us?

Faraj

I kicked my heels impatiently against the wooden legs of Fadi's sofa. He was in a meeting about the London bombing, and I wanted to be there. But he said I wasn't ready. The others had laughed at my suit, called me names they thought I wouldn't understand. But I still spoke my own language, Grandmother and Uncle Massoud spoke Arabic at home.

They thought that I was too weak to believe the way they do, that because I was raised in Canada, I was polluted with ideals that would compromise my faith. They had no idea how much I hated living here. How much I missed my own country, I still remembered it. I remembered my mother.

Fadi poked his head around the corner of the door to his bedroom and waved me over. Finally! They trusted me with their constant secrets, I was going to belong. I was going to help them avenge the murders of our people all those years ago, the deaths of all the martyrs would be made right. We would gain honour for the afterlife, it would be glorious.

But as I stood in the door, stared at coldly by the other men, it seemed more scary than glorious. Fadi was the only one smiling at me, the others scowled coldly into their thin beards.

For the first time I realized that they were barely older than me, they were the age of the six in London. Maybe as few as four years separated us. They didn't look as wise as they had before either, now they looked angry and hate-filled.

Only Fadi still smiled, still looked filled with joy at the thought of doing Allah's work. He clapped me on the shoulder, showing his approval in the face of these dark, angry young men.

"Faraj has come to help us, to join our sacred cause. Isn't that right?" He looked at me and I nodded wordlessly. He smiled encouragingly.

"He's too young." One of the others stated dismissively. "Send the child home."

The others grunted or laughed in agreement. Only Fadi shook his head.

"That's why we need him. He can move around the city without raising suspicion." The others looked doubtful. "Look at him!"

One by one, they nodded. Only one was still scowling ferociously at me. But he was enough. Heavier than the others, his beard was fuller, his brows thicker. I'd seen him around; it was Ali.

After a few moments, Fadi pulled me gently toward the door.

"I have a job for you. Don't concern yourself, it's perfectly innocent. But you must have noticed that the police are now looking at all of us with suspicion. We can barely go to the store for groceries."

I hadn't noticed any such thing, but nodded anyway, I didn't want to look like a dumb kid.

"I just need you to take a package to a friend for me. If you put it in your school bag, they'll never even look at you. Okay?" I nodded slowly.

He walked me to the door of the apartment. I was starting to wonder if I'd gotten in over my head, if the police were stopping Muslim men, just for nothing...

Fadi must have noticed that I was worried, because he bent over a little to look me in the eyes. He smiled encouragingly, seeming to be unaffected by the sour moods and fears of the other men.

"Do not be worried, little friend. The package is not illegal, or important. I just don't want to be questioned. You understand?" I nodded and he grinned brightly, clapping me on the shoulder again. I felt like a puppy who finally remembered how to do his trick.

Samantha

I was definitely not comfortable here.

Carrie Whitehorse wasn't one of Ash's two native friends that I'd met at the school. She was older, hard, cold. I instinctively disliked her, and didn't trust her as far as I could throw her. Overhand.

Ash had taken the money from me as soon as we were out of sight of the house. I was a bit nervous that she'd disappear with it, and that my great experiment in disreputable behaviour would get me in shit for nothing. So I'd insisted on coming with her to get the stuff.

I kind of regretted that now, Carrie scared me. Her eyes seemed to look right through me, like I was nothing.

She pulled Ash close and whispered in her ear, but loudly enough to be sure I heard her.

"Who the hell is she? Are you trying to get me busted?" Ash shook her head.

"She's okay; she lives in Snake's old place."

Carrie didn't look convinced. Maybe she'd hated Snake.

"No, I won't talk to you with her here. Get rid of her, or there's no deal."

Great. There goes my thirty bucks.

Ash looked at me; I could see she wanted me to go, so I shrugged like it meant less than nothing to me. And I walked back out into the crappy, smelly hallway. Hoping that they didn't just sneak out the back door and leave me here.

On the other hand, I was way over my head, I knew it, Carrie knew it, and even through her pain Ash probably knew it. I was seriously starting to be afraid of what I was getting into. Drugs!? This is crazy!

But I was more afraid of looking stupid in front of Ashleigh. She'd tell the whole gang, and my life would get even worse. Though that was hard to picture.

Besides, why bother keeping my nose clean? Why put up with the whispers and name calling at school, I was kidding myself if I thought McGill would give money to someone from Mechanicsville, no matter what their marks were. It would serve my parents right if I became a drug addict prostitute meth dealer. They ruined my life.

I curled my nose at the stink of old urine and something bitter I couldn't identify. It was a bit smoky and dark green smelling, I hoped it wasn't someone's dinner.

I wondered again what was taking so long.

Ashleigh

Carrie didn't trust white girl. I guess I'd gotten so used to seeing her moping around, that I'd forgotten how badly she fit in. Looking at her ironed blouse and Vanderbilt jeans as if I'd never seen them before, I nearly laughed. Did white girl have no idea how dumb that looked around here? It was like screaming "mug me!" on the street. I glanced at Carrie, or yelling "nark!"

"No, I won't talk to you with her here. Get rid of her, or there's no deal." Carrie looked a bit wild behind her eyes, so I nodded at Miss prissy to leave.

I thought for a second that she was going to refuse, but she just looked worried for a moment, and then stepped into the hall. I half expected her to be gone when I came out.

"You shouldn't be bringing strangers to my place. You know better than that, little sister." Carrie was right, I wasn't thinking clearly.

"Sorry, it's just that she had the money, and I was…I really needed to…. Jeff".

To my horror, I started to cry.

Faraj

Fadi certainly looked relaxed. Sitting in the library carrel with his feet up on the chair beside him, reading the paper. He had a pile of books on the table in front of him, but wasn't paying them any attention.

I had a couple of history books under my arm, just for show. I needed a reason to sit at the table next to him.

I walked over nervously, but as I arrived at the carrels, he just glanced at me and dropped his feet to the floor. That was it, not a sign of recognition. He went back to his paper, so I pulled a notebook out of my bag and started doing homework. At least I'd get something out of this.

About forty minutes later, Fadi's cell phone rang. As he talked, he packed up his stuff and disappeared between the stacks. Striving to look casual, I pulled the paper over and thumbed through it. Stuck in by the comics was a note from Fadi.

It said to go to the men's room on the third floor; the package was tucked into the toilet tank of the third stall. I was both thrilled and frightened, I felt like I was in a movie. Carefully checking to see that no-one was watching me, I got up and headed for the third floor. Then I went back, stuffed my books into my backpack and left again.

The bathroom was, thankfully, empty. It was dark and a bit dirty, but I figured that was normal in an old building. I was just lucky nothing was broken or leaking. I stepped into the third stall, feeling very self-conscious.

I carefully locked the door behind me and stared at the old, stained toilet. I had to reach into the tank for whatever it was Fadi had left me? Yuck!

Maybe it wouldn't be as bad as I thought. I quietly lifted the lid from the tank and laid it across the toilet seat. I could see a small package tightly wrapped in a plastic grocery bag, tucked behind the tower thing in the tank. It looked to have a lot of tape on it to keep it sealed. I guessed that it was about the size of a thin paperback book.

I opened the stall door and looked out, still no-one around. I locked the door again. I stared at the greasy looking water in the tank. The package was wedged well underwater, more than halfway down. There was no help for it; I was going to have to reach in.

So I gritted my teeth, pulled up my sleeve, and too quick to think about it, reached in and grabbed the plastic and yanked.

My fingers slipped on the wet surface and my hand flew up to smack me in the chin. My empty hand. I could've screamed in disgust at the slimy water, and now I had to do it again.

So I reminded myself that Fadi had proposed this to prove I was trustworthy. I couldn't shame him, and myself, by being too squeamish to get a bloody book and deliver it. I refused to think of the package as anything but a book.

So, I pulled up my sleeve again, gritted my teeth and stuck my hand in the cold water once more.

The cold slime was gross, but I grasped the package firmly and tugged it. It didn't move. Shit.

Then I thought to tug it sideways, and it slipped free. I pulled it quickly from the tank and yanked off some toilet paper to dry it. There was water soaked into every fold, but it didn't seem to have gotten past the tape. At least I hoped it hadn't.

I sat down to try to dry it off before putting it in with school books. Then the bathroom door opened, and a pair of footsteps came in slowly, quietly. Reflexively, I pulled my feet up and out of sight.

The footsteps checked the length of the bathroom, pausing outside my stall. I held my breath, suddenly convinced that this was a cop. They'd been watching Fadi and the others, he saw me take Fadi's note, and he knew I was in here. He knew I had the package.

He still hadn't moved from in front of my stall. I was starting to see flashy lights and was burning with the desperate need to breathe. Then, thankfully, he moved back to the door.

I inhaled as quietly as I could, fighting the urge to gulp at the air like a drowning man. I started to move my feet back to the floor.

Then the door opened and a second man came in. I yanked my feet back up.

I could hear them approach the sinks. One of them sniffed, and I
wondered if they could smell me. I sweated more just thinking
about that.

Samantha

I looked at my watch again. What was taking so long? Were they growing the pot from seed? I started to feel certain that they had snuck out the back way, leaving me here.

I didn't even know where we were. We'd followed the bike path for awhile, and then gone through a couple of alleys. I hated to admit it, I had zero idea how to get home. I didn't even know if there was a working pay phone in this neighbourhood. Looking around, I had to admit it. I had thought nothing could be worse than the dump I lived in, but I was wrong. This place was worse. Way worse.

Aside from the pee smell that the cracked linoleum gave off, and the broken stair rail and the squishy carpet on the stairs, all the lights were broken. Pretty amazing considering that someone had installed little wire cages around all the light bulbs. I wondered how they got broken. Did someone poke every one with a stick? Wouldn't he have gotten glass in his eyes?

And why would anyone go to that much trouble to make the dark hallway even darker? My imagination came up with a few reasons. All of a sudden I didn't want to know anymore.

A door banged open behind me, making me jump and squeal with fright. But it was only Ash. Suddenly I felt very stupid. Of course she hadn't left me here to get raped and murdered, or eaten by rats. I was such a wuss.

Ashleigh

To apologize for being so paranoid, Carrie gave me a couple of hits off her pipe. She'd mixed something in with the hash; I was already fuzzy around the edges. My head felt like it was trailing behind my body by several feet, making it hard to walk.

White girl looked even whiter than usual, her pale face glowing in the darkened hallway. Her dark blue jeans seemed to fade in and out of existence, blending into the strange blue of the walls, lit only by the streaks of dirty sunlight fighting their way through the cracked windows.

Wow, I should be writing this down; I'd ace the poetry contest at school. It would be published in the yearbook for everyone to see. Maybe I could send it to my dad. I fumbled in my pockets for a pen, but found the bag of pot instead.

"Kwe, hi, kemosabe, how you doing?" I was feeling better, good even. I couldn't wait to find a place to toke up, mellow out, start flying....

I missed what white girl had said. Shit, now I'd have to figure out how to talk again.

"Whazzup?" That was close enough.

"What's up? What do you mean what's up? Did you get it? What took so long? Did you smoke it already?" She leaned over and stared closely at my eyes, going out of focus and making me dizzy. I held up my hands to slow down the flood of questions.

My hands were glowing, casting multiple shadows as they moved. It was so beautiful. White girl grabbed my hand and I realized she'd been talking again. White people sure do talk a lot.

Faraj

"We're alone, I checked."

"Did you check under the stalls?"

There was a shuffling noise. I imagined them staring at my stall as if they could sense me here. My throat got dry, I had to cough. My nose itched. My head was feeling light, and I realized that I'd stopped breathing again.

I thought about those men in London, barely older than me. Would they have been squatting here in fear, trapped in a toilet? No, they'd have been brave. They would've stayed hidden to protect Fadi's package, but they'd have courage in their hearts, not terror. Slowly, my racing heart slowed, its pounding in my ears subsided and I could hear the men more clearly.

Why, they weren't cops. They weren't looking for me; they were doing some sort of drug deal. I almost laughed out loud in relief.

"Do you have the shit?" That was the sniffing one; though he sounded more like he had a cold now.

"Course I do, you got the money?"

"Give it to me."

"Gimme my money first. A thousand bucks, all of it."

"A thousand! I don't owe you shit. Just the forty for this."

"You fucking do! You never paid for that party, man. Remember, what's her name's birthday. You said you'd sell the stuff at the party and pay me after."

"I paid you for that already."

"You paid me twenty bucks, man. That was a thousand worth of shit."

I leaned back as quietly as I could. It looked like they were going to be here awhile.

Samantha

Ashleigh was stoned, I could tell. I hoped she hadn't already smoked it all. It didn't seem fair that I was going to get in trouble for stealing Dad's money and she got to smoke all the pot.

"Whazzup?" She was slurring her words. I felt a rush of anger.

"What's up? What do you mean what's up? Did you get it? What took so long? Did you smoke it already?"

She held up her hands, staring at them as if she's never seen them before. I was torn by relief at seeing the baggie in her hand, and being pissed off at her for leaving me alone while she started the party without me.

And had she ever started! She looked like she could barely walk. This was going to be so much fun. Not!

"Ash, let's go."

"Go?" She seemed puzzled, "Go where?"

"I don't know, home? The school? Bermuda?" I just wanted to get away from here.

"Okay." She grinned sloppily up at me through her lashes. She was still trying to watch her hands, but seemed happy to follow me. Great, she thinks we're going to Bermuda.

I took the baggie and stuffed it in my jacket pocket. I could just picture her waving it around out on the street. If we didn't get arrested, we'd be robbed.

Faraj

I pulled the stall door open and peered out, thankfully they were gone. By now the plastic bag had air dried, so I shoved it into my school bag and hurried out. The library was closing soon, and I didn't want to be found still in the bathroom.

That would draw attention. My nerves couldn't take any attention from suspicious strangers right now. I'd scream and run like a coward, I knew I would.

Two hours sitting in there, my legs going numb, listening to those idiots argue. Now I was going to be late for my curfew, and my uncle would grill me. He was always disapproving of everything I did. Nothing was good enough. If I got an A, it should have been an A+. If I disagreed with him, I was being rude. If I agreed, I was being sarcastic. And he worried all the time about what I was doing, who I was with, even accused me of lying and hiding things.

Of course, I was hiding things from him, but only because he refused to understand my feelings. How could he expect me to be honest with him when he was always telling me what to feel, and what to think?

I'd heard him refer to my mother as "that woman" when he thought I was out of earshot. How could he be so disrespectful after she died in the war against the aggressors? And he was always preaching respect and tolerance at me, where was his tolerance for my beliefs?

I eased the bathroom door open and peered out onto the library floor. Rows of shelves, an empty book cart. No sign of anyone. Good.

Stepping out, I softly closed the door, then tried to walk confidently to the stairs, in case anyone saw me. I reached the stairs without seeing a soul. Was the library already closed? I start to sweat. What if I'm locked in? Fadi would kill me. So would Uncle Mahmoud.

I practically ran down the stairs, feeling both scared of being alone in this spooky old building, and stupid for being afraid.

"No running!" a woman hissed from between the stacks, nearly giving me a heart attack. I spun on one heel and nearly fell down the stairs. My pulse was pounding and I could hardly breathe.

It was an older woman, wearing glasses, and a modest sweater. She was trying so hard not to laugh, but I could see it in her eyes.

I could feel my face burning, and wanted to explain myself, or say something withering. But instead, I just turned and walked slowly down the stairs. The back of my neck burning with embarrassment.

Samantha

Somehow we made it back to the bike path. I had no idea where we were going; I had never been so lost in my life. How could we be fifteen minutes from home, and be so totally lost? I just prayed that Ash knew where we were. No way was I calling my dad to come get me, even if I did find a working pay phone.

After a few minutes' walk, trying to keep Ash upright and moving, we came to the park behind Parliament Hill. Ash giggled as she gave the one finger salute to the House of Commons. I had to admit, they deserved it.

"Fat, middle-aged, white, rich guys. Deciding what's best for my people. Bastiches!" Ash wasn't in a happy mood anymore. I wondered what the government had done to her.

I mean, I knew about the blankets infected with smallpox in the seventeen hundreds, and the residential schools they were forced into in the fifties. But Ash was my age, what had they done to her?

We walked a little farther, until she stopped dead in her tracks, staring at the cliff under the Canadian Mint's backside. Then she started laughing. At nothing. Laughing so hard she choked and turned red in the face.

I was pounding her back when she looked at me and started laughing again. Great.

Then she started turning in slow circles. I was seriously reconsidering this whole adventure. I sure as hell didn't want to be

a stoned as she was. I yelled at her to calm down, to stop acting so
v eird, there were other people here.

Then she just... stopped. Shaking her head, she seemed almost
n ormal again. A bit tipsy, but almost normal.

Ashleigh

I wondered why white girl had brought me to Parliament Hill. It seemed a pretty risky place to toke up; I mean the RCMP would be all over the place. Then I saw the House of Commons building.

I'd gone there with my group from the Odawa Native Friendship Centre last year to protest the proposed changes to the Indian Act. That was an interesting afternoon. I had cuffed school for the day and gone to paint posters at the centre. They seemed glad to have my help, I felt accepted there, important.

Not like at school, or home. But I didn't want to think about home, so I just gave the finger to the Indian Affairs minister for reminding me of Jeff and kept walking.

It was really beautiful down here. The Ottawa river was high, and there were ducks floating placidly along, looking for tourists to mug for bread scraps. The bank on this side of the river had a cement bike path meandering along, dotted with little islands, each possessing an old fashioned looking lamp post, two scroll-work iron benches and a garbage can in a decorative matching iron cover. It looked like a movie set for a tasteful romance film. Maybe something with Jodie Foster in it.

Then I spotted the opening of the old gold mine beneath the Canadian Mint. I used to go there a couple of years ago to explore. It was closed with a metal gate, but if they hadn't fixed it since I was there last, we could still slip in. What a perfect place to hide out for the afternoon.

We could pretend we were shamans, from before the white man came. Sitting in a sacred cave, dreaming the future. Well, as long a white girl kept quiet, no way she could swing being a shaman. I giggled. White girl as a shaman. I could picture her letting someone paint her face with white clay and red ochre, right over her perfect, blond nose.

She stared at me, her eyebrows pushed together. She looked like a worried hamster. That did it, I bent over, laughing so hard I couldn't breathe. I nearly threw up, I laughed so hard. Pinpricks of black stared at me in the corners of my vision. They sparkled. I stopped laughing to stare at them, but they moved when I turned my head, always out of reach.

I turned around, trying to catch them, but they winked out. Gone. So sad, I liked them.

White girl was talking again, pulling at my arm. Now she looked like an angry hamster. So I tried to straighten out.

CHAPTER FOUR

Now it's trouble

Samantha

Ash pushed, then tugged on the piece of metal mesh fence that ran across the opening to the old mine. I felt sure this was a dumb idea, but it was easier to just go along with it. Besides, I wanted her off the public path, she looked really stoned. I wondered what she'd taken at Carrie's. I felt insulted and left out. I felt relieved that I wasn't about to smoke it.

"They must've made the hole smaller." Ashleigh grunted, tugging hard at the wire mesh. Sure they did. Lord knows you couldn't have gotten bigger. Couldn't have like, developed tits or anything.

Okay, so I was starting to feel a bit bitchy. The mosquitoes were out this close to the water. And I was late getting home, my mom would be pissed. Somehow I'd figured this whole thing would only take an hour and we'd be back at the building before anyone noticed I was gone. My parents were really freaked out at the thought of my being outside after dark in our neighbourhood, like I was going to be murdered ten feet from our door.

Of course, I was way more than ten feet from the door now. Parliament Hill was fifteen to twenty minutes away by car, but the bike path was shorter.... I was late. And itchy. And now Ash had disappeared. Fuck!

Of course, I knew she had just squeezed into the mine. But she was gone so fast.

I tried to be gentle and dignified climbing in, but I had a hard time getting through the broken gate without ripping my shirt. There was a piece of the crossbar broken right at boob level, like it was on purpose. But I finally made it, and while my shirt had rust flakes on it, I didn't think I'd ruined it.

I heard Ashleigh call me, but I was still trying to get up the nerve to do this. It wasn't like she was going anywhere without me, how hard could it be to find her in a cave?

I turned and peered out into the lengthening shadows. Five-ish, I thought. I needed to be home in an hour for dinner. Should be ok, a few minutes to smoke the stuff in the baggie, get a little mellow, then head home. If I can manage to look, and smell, okay maybe Ash can stay overnight.

I turned to follow Ash, but it was pitch black after the brightness outside. Really black, like total black. I put my hands out and started shuffling my feet, looking for a wall to follow. I was afraid that if I tripped, I'd split my head open on a rock. And Ashleigh was more likely to play in brains and blood than get help, at least, right now. She'd get help if she was straight. I think.

I couldn't believe that Ash had managed to go anywhere in here; I couldn't see my hand in front of my face! I started to panic. I'm not proud, but there it is. I felt like I was buried in here, lost and forgotten. We would never find our way out.

I was maybe five steps into the darkness, I knew I was being stupid. But my pulse pounded in my ears, and I felt dizzy, like there was no blood getting to my head. I found the wall, and let my left hand trail along it, my right hand held out to look for more walls, or rocks blocking the tunnel. I heard a faint noise from up ahead, like a rat. Or a ghost hand sliding along the rock wall.

"Ash?" I hated how my voice sounded, like I was half whispering because I was terrified. I drew a deep breath. I was not a stupid, half-naked, blond, bimbo in a horror movie. There was nothing ahead of me. Nothing.

Ashleigh

Finally!

I nearly fell down when the rusty fence let go, but I could fit through the opening. I slipped in excitedly; I hadn't been here in years. I used to find the occasional fleck of gold before; I wondered if I would this time? I'd heard that they were thinking of reopening the mine, they hadn't closed it because it was out of gold, it was because it cost too much to get the gold out. But new technology made it easier and cheaper to get the gold.

Their first step was to make it illegal to go swimming near the mine, because they were afraid you'd find bits of gold near the overflow valves from when they used to clean something or other. Apparently bits of gold would wash out too, and collectors could sometimes find it in the river. And they were trying to sell salvage rights to some corporation from the States.

But like, who'd be swimming in that river now? The sewage plant overflowed into it at least twice a month. Yuck!

It was darker in here than outside. I should've brought a flashlight. But I figured I could still find my way around the corner, out of sight from the path. Who needed light to smoke up anyway?

I patted my pockets but didn't find the baggie. Shit! No, wait. White girl took it. Where was she?

"White girl?" My voice echoed eerily in the blackness. She didn't respond.

"This isn't funny. You got the stuff." I waited, listening. There was no sound at all, not even breathing. She hadn't even come in. Was she afraid of the dark?

I found that pretty funny, Miss Too Good for You is afraid of the dark. Then I heard her coming, dragging her feet to avoid tripping over something, breathing loud in the silence. I could picture her hands stretched out in front of her, trying to feel her way through the darkness.

"Ash?" Her voice was quiet, strangled. She sounded like she was getting freaked out. Oh, I knew it was mean, I knew I shouldn't, but I couldn't stop myself.

I waited until she was almost at the point that the tunnel branched, she was only feet away, and I jumped out in front of her, a war cry ululating from my throat.

Her scream was terrified, and then she started cursing like a gang banger. I couldn't stop laughing. I knew I should apologize, but I couldn't get any words out. Finally the curses wound down, and I was able to draw a full breath and make myself stop laughing.

"Very funny." But she didn't sound amused, she sounded very angry. All of a sudden, I really was sorry. I felt around in front of me until I caught her arm.

"I'm sorry pale face, I was just kidding. I didn't mean to scare you... exactly." I thought about it for a second. "Well, I did mean to scare you, just not that much.... It seemed funny."

I heard her sigh, sounding just like my mother.

"It's okay, Ash." Then she snorted, "It probably was pretty funny."

I laughed again, relieved that she wasn't mad any more. I told myself that it was just because she had the baggie. But I was actually starting to like her, she was so... open. She was honest about shit, like she didn't play the head games the others were always into, trying to see who was smarter, like any of them had a future.

But white girl could have a future, she might be street dumb, but she was book smart. The kind who went to University and became lawyers. I wondered if she was gay. I could pretend to be gay if it got me out of my dead-end life. At least long enough to get alimony.

"Hey, Ash. Have you got any papers or matches? I mean, we have to make those little cigarette things, right?"

Cigarette things? Had she never seen a joint before?

"Yeah, Carrie always gives me some papers and matches with the grass. She says it's all part of the A+ service."

I wished I could see her face, but I could barely see her silhouette, the light was fading fast outside the mine entrance.

"Let's go around the corner so the light from the matches can't be seen outside." I searched for white girl's hand. She jumped a little when I touched her, but didn't say anything. She just took my hand and followed me.

It was so trusting, so sweet, like a baby. I felt tears sting my eyes, but I refused to cry. It's just coming down from … whatever that was I took. I'll be better as soon as I toke up.

Samantha

I didn't like it. The smoke was really acrid, burning not just my lungs, but my throat and eyes as well. I couldn't stop coughing to catch my breath and Ash laughed at me for wasting the smoke.

A few minutes later I started to feel light, not just light-headed but light all over. Like I was going to float away

I looked around me, trying to see the source of the sparkly lights in this pitch dark cave, listening to Ash talk about what she was going to do to Jeff the next time he fell asleep on the couch. Ash was waxing poetic about her revenge on Jeff, though I still wasn't quite sure if he'd succeeded in raping her or not. Her plans became more and more outlandish; from Bobbitizing him and shoving his severed penis up his butt hole, to forcing him to give old lady Perkins's dog a blow job. We were laughing like fools. I never thought she could be serious.

After a while we were quiet. I could hear water drops ringing like bells somewhere in the dark. There was a scuffling noise in the distance; I figured it was a squirrel stashing nuts in the giant hole left by the miners. I smiled at the thought of a ton of nuts lost in the inky darkness, the squirrel forever wondering where they'd gone.

"I told my mom."

It took me a moment to remember what Ash was talking about. Then I was disappointed. I'd expected that if Ash's mom had any idea what Jeff was trying to do, that there would have been screaming, cop cars, probably an ambulance. But I'd heard nothing.

"What did she do?"

"Grounded me."

"What? She didn't believe you?" I was stunned. We might fight, but my mom would always take my side, I knew it. It was as normal as the sun setting.

"She believed me, but Jeff said I did it to him when he was drinking, so that I could break them up."

I wondered what it must be like, to be forced to do something horrible and have your own mother think it was your fault.

But Ashleigh just snorted, like it was what she expected.

CHAPTER FIVE

Home Again

Samantha

I was starving.

I abandoned Ash on the first floor with unseemly haste and headed upstairs, hoping to find something in the fridge I didn't have to cook first. I could hear voices in the hall, and as I got closer I recognized mom's voice. The other person turned out to be Faraj's grandmother, tonight wearing a cotton tunic and pants with flowers embroidered around the edges.

They were laughing, at least until mom got a sniff of me. Her eyes narrowed so quickly I thought they were going to disappear altogether. Fortunately for me, Mrs. Qahhar starting talking again, and mom was too polite to interrupt her to grill me.

I pored over the sad remains in our fridge and decided to make a sandwich. At least we had ketchup. As I stood at the table putting it together, I could hear them still talking in the hall.

I sat quietly and listened, they were talking about Faraj.

"He is very much like his mother, him. Very angry with the world. But he is a good boy."

"What happened to his mother?"

"She died." It sounded very final to me, but mom didn't let it alone.

"Was she killed in the war, like his father?"

"No, not like my son." There was a pause, the kind you can feel. I thought I could sense her mind moving back to when Faraj's father was still alive. "Not like my son at all."

"It must have been very difficult for him, losing both parents, moving here."

"He was too young to remember his mother, I don't know why he is so like her. So... impetuous."

"How old was he when you moved here?"

"He was eight, we thought it a good thing to move away from the wars and anger. Perhaps we brought it with us. Perhaps it is in our genes to be angry and hateful."

"That's just exhaustion talking, it must be so hard raising a teenager at your age. It's hard enough raising one at mine."

And that brought her thoughts back to me, and my weed smelly jacket. I could tell by her tone, and was surprised when she changed the subject instead of coming in.

"I really need a cup of tea and a change of scenery. Would you like to come with me? There's a lovely little place up on Preston."

I sat there, picking crumbs off my empty plate long after mom and Mrs. Qahhar had gone out. The light moved across the table and my plate, flaring brightly where it hit mom's silver butter knife. I was thinking deep, portentous thoughts about the parallels between Faraj and myself.

We'd both been taken from our homes, stripped of everything familiar and safe, ending up in this hell-hole ghetto. I didn't mean belittle his experience, it was way worse than losing your fancy school and swimming pool, but still, it felt the same to me. I felt like I was forgetting who I was. Only while I was writing did I still feel like me. I was accustomed to being special, but here... well, here nobody cared. Here I had to be someone alien; tougher, angrier, and more cynical.

But Faraj had lost everything; his family, his country, his language and culture. My feeling of alienation was probably nothing compared to his.

Poor baby, I bet I could make him feel better. I could... better not go there. Mom would freak if she even thought I was thinking of that. I started to giggle, I couldn't help myself.

Faraj

Arriving home was every bit as strained as I'd feared. First Uncle Massoud demanded to know where I'd gone after school, and then didn't believe I'd been to the library because I had no library books and no work done. And I certainly couldn't tell him about hiding in the bathroom for two hours.

"You must apply yourself, Faraj. There will be time for other things when you are settled in a good career."

"I do apply myself; I have some of the best marks in my class."

"No-one will give you anything for free in this country, nephew. You have two things against you, you are brown and you are Muslim. People will try to hold you down because of these things. You must work harder and be more polite and more..."

I tuned him out. He was always saying how bad things were for us here, but his solution was just to be patient and put up with the abuse. Why didn't he ever think of standing up for himself? Or fighting back?

"I worry about you Faraj. There are many temptations for a young man out there. And you never talk to me."

"Well, you can stop worrying, uncle. The girls around here don't interest me at all." Great, now he was going to give me the sex talk. Again.

I got up off the bed and checked the hall again. I could still hear the TV going in the living room, but I was feeling paranoid. I looked at Fadi's package lying on the striped coverlet. It was still

98

wrapped in the plastic grocery bag. It seemed to be bigger than it was at the library. More menacing.

He'd told me to take the outer wrapping off, and there I would find the name and address of the person I was to give it to. I walked over slowly and picked it up. It was still about the size and weight of a paperback novel, but that didn't make sense. Why so much secrecy over a book? It had to be something else. But I'd never figure it out staring at the wrapping.

And Fadi had said that I was not to peek at the item itself, I was just to deliver it. This was a test of my loyalty, to see if I would follow directions. It was a way to prove myself to the others. But as eager as I had been before, now I wasn't so sure.

I started to shake it, and then thought better, what if it exploded? I didn't believe Fadi was into anything that dangerous, but still.

It could be a book on a watch list. One about martyrs, or tactics, or something.

Samantha

The next day I was sitting on the steps, trying to get some air while working on my math homework. It was hard to concentrate; my eyes were itchy, and burning. I figure it was from the pot yesterday. And it was another muggy day, with all the car fumes hovering at street level, making it feel like there was no oxygen in the air.

The door closed with a bang behind me. I ignored it, thinking it would be mom with another lecture about Ash and the dangers of drugs. It was only once, for Pete's sakes. And just weed, it wasn't like I did crystal meth.

But it wasn't my mom. It was Faraj.

He was dressed casually, but neatly. His black hair shone in the sun. He was "to die for" gorgeous. As always.

This time he wasn't as calm as usual. He looked like he needed to talk, and I guess I was the only one around. He just stared at his shoes for a moment, then picked some invisible lint from his sleeve.

"Are you okay, Faraj? Is something wrong?" I probably should have let him speak first, but patience was never my strong suit.

He shrugged and I figured that would be the end of it. I blew my one chance to really talk to him. I'm such a loser.

When he was still silent several minutes later, I picked up my books to leave. I could be rejected and ignored in my own home; I didn't need it out here too.

"Please wait." His voice was quiet, and uncertain. "May I ask you a question?"

I turned around as casually as I could, I didn't want to look eager. After a moment I shrugged, like it didn't make no never mind to me. That's the way my grandmother always put it. God I missed her. She'd died near Christmas two years ago. She'd been my closest friend, my biggest fan, my...

Faraj had obviously asked me his question and I'd missed it. Shit!

"Do you think I should? Or should I just trust him?"

Damn, I had no idea what he was talking about. But I couldn't admit I hadn't been listening, I'd rather die. So, I decided to fake it.

"Well, has he ever done anything to make you not trust him?"

"No, but I didn't know him when this happened last time. He might be involved. But do I have the right to doubt him? This could be nothing."

Okay, now I was really lost.

How do I fake my way out of this?

Ashleigh

My head felt like it was stuffed with sand. My eyes were where the sand spilled out, gritty and red. I'd never gotten a hangover from weed before. Again I wondered what that was that Carrie'd given me to smoke.

I had to pee, so I struggled to get out of bed. Somehow the sheets had gotten tangled around my feet and I couldn't untangle them. Finally I just kicked the whole mess off the foot of the bed.

I bumped into Jeff as I came out of the bathroom. Literally. He must've been waiting for me.

He grabbed my arms, squeezing until it hurt. I just stared at him, refusing to show fear or pain. I figured he was like a cowardly dog, they can tell if you're weak or scared, and that gives them the courage to attack.

"You came in awfully late last night, little girl. You know what the punishment is for that?"

I tried to pull my arms free, but he squeezed tighter, watching my eyes for a reaction He pushed me up against the bathroom door, leaning in close enough for me to smell the sour stink of his skin.

"Your mama was worried about you. You're a bad girl, worrying your mama."

"My mom was at work until two, I was in before midnight."

"You don't be giving me lip." He shook me, like I was rag doll. "You better learn to respect me."

I think I lost it, I don't remember what I said or did, just the blood pounding in my ears, and my head ringing. Next thing I knew, my nose was bleeding and my t-shirt was ripped. Jeff was on the floor, curled up and swearing a blue streak. I don't think I'd ever heard some of those combinations before. But I knew better than to stay and listen. As soon as he could get to his feet again, I was in real shit.

I raced to my room to grab my pants, nearly falling in my haste to get into them. I grabbed my purse and headed straight for the door. I had no idea where to go.

Faraj

I didn't even know why I was talking to her. It was obvious she wasn't listening, and I didn't dare give her enough information to make her opinion worth anything anyway. I guess I just needed to talk to someone, so I could hear my voice say the words. Except that I didn't dare say the words. This was pointless.

I opened my mouth to say something so I could leave. Apologize for wasting her time probably, between Uncle Massoud and Fadi, it was a wonder I didn't apologize for breathing.

Samantha looked at me and blushed; I guessed that she realized that she'd been ignoring me. Before either of us could say anything, the front door slammed open and the girl from the first floor came flying out. She ran right into us, knocking me off the steps, so that I fell and tore the knee of my pants.

Samantha was knocked onto her seat, and she just sat there, looking stunned. But the other girl just got up and ran. It was like she hadn't even noticed us.

"Ash!" Samantha called to her, and then started racing after her. "Ash, wait up!"

I was left alone with my scraped knee. Then I realized that the girls had given me my answer. They were unworthy vessels for the Almighty to speak through, but they carried his message none-the-less.

Samantha's loyalty to her friend was all important. Despite being already occupied with me, she was willing to dump everything for her friend's needs. As I must do for Fadi's needs.

I went back upstairs to open the package and get the address. I would deliver it right away, before they started wondering why I was taking so long. It didn't matter what was in it, I was to be there for my friend's needs. And they needed me to deliver Fadi's package without questions.

I said I would do it; I was going to do it. But I was not happy about it. The outside wrapping was crumpled on my bed, beside the still wrapped package from Fadi. I looked at the name and address again, hoping that the person I was to deliver it to had somehow changed. But of course, it hadn't.

Ali Faloul Saddique, the Mullah's son. Shit.

I knew what this was. It was part of the test. Fadi knew that Ali hated me, and didn't want me involved. He wanted to see if I'd be willing to do something I didn't want to do, in order to be a part of things. I understood that, a part of being a man was being able to do unpleasant things. But Ali *really* hated me.

I just knew that he'd make a big deal over my not delivering the package last night, right after I picked it up, and he'd have no patience for excuses. Everything I could say would just make me look worse.

Well, I had to do it, so I might as well just get to it. Just breathe deep, and do it. So why was I still sitting on my bed looking at Ali's name? Because I'm an idiot.

I forced myself to get up, change my slacks, and pull my jacket out of the closet. I'd better look as non-threatening as possible. Not give Ali anything else to criticize.

I put the package back into my school bag and shouldered it. I'd have to tell Grandmother that I was going to the library, so I'd better remember to stop off there to take out a couple of books, or Uncle Massoud would accuse me of lying again.

I got mad just remembering the argument we'd had. It didn't matter that I was lying and sneaking around; he had no right to call me a liar! How dare he not trust me? How could he insult me like that?

I didn't run into either my uncle or my grandmother on the way out of the building, and I took that as a sign that I was doing the right thing. I also caught the bus at the corner without having to wait more than a couple of minutes, another good sign. Maybe this would be okay. Maybe Ali wouldn't be as harsh as I expected him to be. I was starting to feel better about the whole thing.

Samantha

I'd never seen anyone so scared. Ash didn't even notice that she'd ploughed right over us. I took off after her, she had trouble, and I was betting it was Jeff. She *had* to call the cops.

I pounded down the pavement after her, too winded to call her name again. Man, she was in good shape; I couldn't believe that she could run like this without ever attending gym class.

Finally, I had to stop, I couldn't breathe and my side was killing me. It took all I had to try yelling one more time.

"Ash, stop!"

To my great surprise, she did.

"Oh, white girl. I thought it was…" She walked back to me, barely winded.

"Jeff." I nodded, wheezing. "You okay?"

She nodded, peering down the street behind us. I noticed that her hair was uncombed, falling in a tangled mass. Her eyes were red-rimmed, like she'd been crying. It was kind of sad to see her acting like nothing was wrong, as if I couldn't see for myself.

"This time we have to call the police." As she shook her head, I pressed on. "I'm serious, who knows what he's going to do to you. I don't want to find your dead body in the dumpster next time I take out the garbage."

She shook her head again, but seemed less certain. Maybe I was getting through to her.

"We can tell my mom. She'll call the cops, they'll believe her." Ash turned away and started walking. I tried to keep up with her and keep talking at the same time, I was in rough shape. I got winded in no time flat.

"Ash, wait. My mom saw the bruises. Even if they won't believe that he…" I didn't want to say it out loud. Actually, I didn't know if he had, you know. Not for sure.

"Wait…. They'll believe my mom that he's been beating you up, and that's a crime too. It'll at least get him out of the house."

She spun around to glare at me, hair flying wildly.

"Unless they take me out of the house. Put me in a group home that's worse than juvie." She looked sullen, the black eye more green than purple now.

"You think the cops are going to believe I didn't deserve this when Jeff gets done talking to them?"

"That's my point Ash; it doesn't matter if you deserved it. It's still a crime to hit you."

"Oh, so now you think I deserve it? I thought you were my friend!"

Ash just stomped off, ignoring my calling after her. I felt betrayed; she knew that wasn't what I'd meant. I knew she was upset, but lashing out at me when I was trying to help was just mean.

I turned around to go home. I just didn't get what Ashleigh was doing this for. How could she blame me for trying to help? Fine, to hell with her. Maybe she liked it. It just wasn't my problem. My problem was getting into a good university and away from this hell-hole. Ash was just a distraction, she was slowing me down. From now on, it was me first, everyone else a dim second.

I told myself that it was my choice and I felt better for making it. Looking after number one, and all that.

But I still felt crappy. I went home anyway.

CHAPTER SIX

Deeper and Darker

Ashleigh

Well, that was stupid. I had panicked, attacking Sam when she just wanted to get Jeff thrown in jail. But I knew that the cops would side with him, not me.

Jeff had told me so. Over and over and over, he knew cops. They'd believe him. They all knew my record, assault, possession, theft.... I'd be the one sent up, not him. He'd come out smelling like a rose. Even my mom believed him.

So, I couldn't let the paleface tell anyone what was going on. Although I desperately wanted to believe that she could make it stop.

No, I was better off on my own. The pain of hoping it would get better, and then things not changing except to get worse, hurt more than what Jeff was doing. I'd just have to stay away from the apartment, away from Jeff and the hell away from white girl, with her white middle-class law-abiding morality. She just didn't understand anything.

I only noticed I was crying when I saw my reflection in a store window. I hated myself for feeling anything. I needed some more stuff, to make me numb.

Samantha

No-one was around when I got home. The whole building was quiet, like it had been abandoned. I figured that would be just my luck, some epidemic sweeps through the city, the military forcing citizens to flee ahead of it, and I'm not home. Nobody even left me a note.

"Sorry not to wait for you, dear. But by the time you see this note, you'll probably already be infected. Please die in the bath tub so there's less mess to clean up when we return. Love mom"

But I knew I was just avoiding the question of what I should do now. I'd actually wanted to talk to my parents, probably for the first time in a month, but they weren't here. I could try calling Ash's mother, but she was probably at work, and Ash said that she was on Jeff's side, anyway.

I could call the police, but if Ash came home and saw the car waiting, she'd probably just run away. Back to Carrie's, or worse. She might go to see her father in prison. Or just disappear.

I felt six years old again. I just wanted my mom to come home. I was too young for this much pressure, I didn't know what to do. I wished my grandmother was still alive.

Faraj

I could hear the music from home through the closed door. It made me homesick, and I thought of my mother. I could almost smell the jasmine scented soap that she liked to use. I knew that this was her way of letting me know I was doing the right thing. She was proud of me.

So, I knocked, loudly enough to be heard over the music.

After a few seconds the music was turned down and footsteps approached the door. I took a deep breath, I wanted to look confident. But I was really hoping that Ali didn't answer the door.

Fate did not listen to me; Ali scowled down at me like I was a bug he wanted to crush under his shoe. I kept my eyes up and back straight, I was here. I had nothing to apologize for.

"I expected you last night."

"I had to go straight home from the library or I would have been late. I didn't want my uncle questioning me about where I was. Fadi said the most important thing was to seem as if everything was normal, and to do nothing strange or unusual."

He glared at me, then just turned and walked away, leaving the door open. I knew then that nothing I ever said or did would change how much he hated me. And my glib remarks only made it worse.

Slowly, I entered the apartment.

I stood awkwardly by the door while Ali went into the other room to get my next delivery. I felt as if he was still watching me, glaring at me like he wanted me dead. I couldn't figure out why Fadi liked and trusted him. He made me think of a serial killer. One of the really gruesome ones.

I wondered what was taking him so long. My nervousness was starting to fade, and curiosity was taking its place. For someone who swore he hated the western world and all of its materialistic greed, he sure owned a lot of nice stuff.

I thought about his passionate speeches against slipping into complacency, against beginning to act and believe like the enemies of our people. I had to admit, his big plasma TV and home theatre setup confused me. Was this where all the money I had worked and sacrificed to give Fadi had gone?

Ali came back while I was standing in front of his DVD collection.

"Did you find what you're looking for?" Ali sounded quietly furious.

"I was just looking around. I was bored." I shrugged, like I hadn't noticed anything off about his apartment.

"This stuff makes me blend in, that is all. When we are ready to move forward, it will all be sold to raise money. Does that make you feel better, child?" He sounded defensive.

"Sure, you'll get a lot for that TV." I couldn't help thinking that he'd never get half of what he paid for it.

He glared at me for a minute, as if he could hear what I was thinking. Then he held out a backpack.

"Take this."

I reached out and took it. It was heavier than it looked, and Ali snorted as it dragged my arm down.

"Are you sure you are big enough for this? Perhaps you should go home to play with your blocks," I knew he was just trying to goad me into losing my temper, testing me, and it still nearly worked. I bit back my reply with an effort.

"I'm fine, Ali. Where do you want me to take it?"

Samantha

Mom and dad finally showed up. They'd been shopping for groceries and were both in a bad mood. We used to love picking out groceries for the next week, back when we could afford to eat.

So the timing really sucked to tell them about Jeff, but I really felt I had no choice. It was an emergency. So I took a deep breath and walked up to Mom.

"Good, you're here. Sam, put this in the fridge." She handed me a bag of carrots that were a bit past their prime and some questionable potatoes.

"Mom, I need to…"

"This, too." Dad handed me a carton of milk and a block of cheese.

"Okay, but I really need …" I turned to open the fridge. I heard the sound of something falling onto the floor.

"Samantha, would you pay attention to what you're doing!" My mom glared at the tub of margarine rolling toward my feet from where she'd dropped it.

"I was putting things in the fridge like you told me to. Besides, it's in a tub, it's fine."

"That's not the point, the point is…"

"The point is I came in here to talk to you about a matter of life and death and you've totally acted like I'm not here except to make me put away stuff that's too crappy to eat anyway!"

"Samantha Hunter, don't you dare yell at me! We're doing the best that we can with very little. And with no appreciation or support from you."

"This is a great time to criticize me, Harriet. Don't you think I'm trying my best?" Now my dad was yelling at my mom, great. So much for either of them listening to me.

"Well, your best doesn't look too damn good, does it?"

"It might look better if you weren't always sabotaging everything I do. Like stealing money to buy God knows what."

"What the hell are you talking about?"

I decided that was my cue to sneak out. They didn't even notice.

I paused outside Ash's door. I should check to see if she came back. But it sounded pretty silent when I bent over to listen at the keyhole. I straightened up again, I sure didn't want to be caught sneaking around like this. Not by Mom and Dad, not by Ash. Certainly not by Faraj, he was just starting to fall under my spell.

Ashleigh

I found myself outside Carrie's door without any idea how I'd gotten there. I could hear her talking to someone, a man from the deep voice. I didn't know whether to knock or not. Carrie liked to keep her customer list secret; she said we'd have less to sell to the cops if we were ever picked up.

I decided to wait down the hall. I could hear the guy leave, but Carrie would see that I wasn't watching to see who it was.

But just as I started to turn around, the door opened and I was face to face with Jeff.

"What are you doing here? Are you following me?" He had the nerve to sound affronted, as if I gave a shit what he was up to. As if I didn't know he was a drug addict loser.

But Carrie was my friend, how could she do this to me?

"How could you sell to *him*?! I thought we were friends!"

Carrie looked stunned at my outburst, but I didn't bother to explain, I just turned to run. But Jeff grabbed my arm, squeezing it painfully as he leaned into my face, his breath pungent with the weed.

"What're you doing here, little girl?" His words were slurred, slow. I knew I was in real trouble if he got me alone. When he was stoned he didn't seem to feel pain, it made him harder to fight off.

"Wait a minute. *This* is the bastard that…" Carrie looked furious. But I didn't have time to think about it, I had to get Jeff off me.

I tried to twist my arm out of his grip, like I saw on TV, then I tried to stamp on his foot, but neither worked. He just hung on, leering at me.

"Did you come to see me, Pocahontas? Are you going to be nice to me for a change?"

"Let go of me, you pig!" My voice was thick with tears, but I didn't know if I was crying in fear or anger.

"Hey, asshole let her go." Carrie waded into the middle like a linebacker in a championship game. But I didn't think it would help, she was skinny, and strung out. Jeff had a good forty pounds on her.

But she went straight for his eyes, fighting like a wild cat. Jeff let go of me to defend himself and Carrie yelled at me to run. I was scared of what he'd do to her for helping me, but ran anyway.

Samantha

I sat on the front porch trying to figure out what to do now. Or where to go to hide out from my parents. It wouldn't be long before they figured out that I'd taken the money, and mom would remember the day I'd come back stinking of pot smoke. Then they'd kill me.

Or worse, sit me down for one of those earnest and heartfelt "where did we go wrong" talks. I'd rather they beat me. Well, maybe not really, but I just hated their talks. They always made me feel so guilty for disappointing them, even if it wasn't my fault.

But this was my fault, so I already felt bad. And they would just try to act like it was their entire fault, like they'd failed me by not teaching me right from wrong. And I'd feel worse.

Now I was starting to get mad.

They were always trying to manipulate me into being the person they thought I should be instead of just letting me be me. Why were parents never happy with who you really were? Why couldn't they love me the way I was? Ignoring the voice that said I hadn't been very lovable lately, I stomped off down the street.

They had no right to treat me this way, and I wasn't going to take it.

Faraj

"So what are you waiting for? Your mother to come hold your hand?"

I had to grit my teeth to keep from cursing him, and I couldn't be polite. Not even to pass this test, the bastard knew about my mother. He knew that was my reason for wanting to be one of them. And he was using her to…

I reined in my temper with great difficulty. I even tried to sound patient, though I probably just sounded pained.

"I'm waiting for you to tell me who to take this to."

"Where, not who." That wasn't any help, but since he was obviously toying with me, trying to get me to lose it, I ignored the urge to punch him right in his smirking mouth. Well, after I'd relished the image for a moment, I ignored it.

He looked disappointed at my non-reaction. Good.

"I want you to take this to the Ottawa Central Bus Depot and put it in locker six hundred. Then give the key to Fadi. You'll have to check it every night at nine and put in more money if it's still there. He may not be able to pick it up right away."

"Because they're watching him? Won't they notice me, if I go there every day but don't pick this up again?"

"Why would they pay attention to you? You're nothing." He waited for a beat to see if I'd react, then sighed. "Go, you have your orders. And remember, if anyone stops you, you had better not mention any of us. We know how to deal with traitors."

"How can they stop me, if I'm too unimportant for them to notice?"

It wasn't much of a comeback, but it annoyed him to have his words thrown back at him, so I was satisfied as I walked out and banged the door behind me.

I knew it was stupid to piss him off, Ali was important in the community, but he was such a … I couldn't think of anything to call him. I'd never met anyone before who could make me so angry by just looking at me. Even the racists at school didn't teach me to hate the way Ali did.

I didn't understand how he could be on the same path to glory as my mother, he was nothing like her. He was rude, arrogant and, well, mean. My mother was courageous and determined. And she never bought herself a fifty-five inch plasma TV.

CHAPTER SEVEN

Alone

Ashleigh

I headed down by the Rideau Centre; I figured I could hide out with the street kids in the Market. Maybe hustle for a little cash, get away from here. I tried not to think of where I could go, since I didn't have anywhere to go.

I walked quickly past all of the stores, back-to-school sales displays bright with promise of a new and better year, but only if you buy their binders and pens. What a load of crap.

And who in their right mind would dress like that for school? That mannequin would get the piss kicked out of her and her lunch stolen by the end of first period. I felt a little better, picturing the blond perfect mannequin having her fancy new jacket stolen.

I turned off the main drag by the bank, and followed the little alley to the parking garage. I knew I could find a couple kids from the northern reservations there. The native kids looked out for each other.

I wondered if I could get back to my Dad's reservation. Tyendenaga Mohawk Territory was a good four hours away by bus; I wondered what a ticket would cost. I could hitchhike, I guess, but there were so many creeps around these days, and the way my luck was running, I'd be picked up by every one of them.

Sure enough, there was the usual native gang splayed over the sidewalk in front of the long abandoned fabric store. From there, they could beg change from the harried businessmen and bored shop clerks as they came from the garage or the bus stop. Some days the money could be okay. Not as good as by the Westin, but the competition was fiercer there. Fierce enough to have killed a boy last summer.

He'd been a junkie, so it might have been drug related, rather than just poaching someone's spot. But I remember the way the cops cracked down on all the kids after that. Especially the Natives and Blacks. Because nice white kids couldn't be killers, could they? Even homeless, desperate ones.

Samantha

I was walking in the general direction of the Queensway, the piece of highway that bisected Ottawa east to west. The only road in the city where the speed limit was 100kph and everyone drove at 80. Everywhere else it was just the reverse.

It was illegal to walk or hitchhike on the Queensway, so I had no idea why I was headed there. I guess it just seemed as good a place to go as any, since there wasn't a 'nowhere' in Ottawa. At least, none that were as nowhere as where I was running away from.

The cars seemed to flash by with little notice of me walking alongside them. I had to keep pulling my attention back to the road, since the one time I stepped out to cross against a light, I nearly got run over. Bastiche didn't even slow down to see if he'd hit me.

I decided I liked that word. It sounded... exotic. Naughty. I wondered where Ash had gotten it, was it Native like her dad? It sounded French.

I wondered briefly how I'd get home. I was not sure how far I'd walked, and the Queensway went all the way through the city. Then I decided I was better off staying away. If I was gone long enough, they'd be too worried to yell at me much. At least for tonight, tomorrow they'd forget how scared they were and start back at me.

I hate my life.

Ashleigh

After the fifth asshole mistook me for a hooker, I decided to give up. This was not my day for panhandling. One of the younger guys seemed to have a knack for it, though. He bought us all donuts for supper.

Everyone agreed the kid had the touch, and there was some talk of sending him to the Westin for the after dinner crowd, but nothing came of it. We were just still too freaked out about that kid last year.

As it got dark, they pulled out their stashes of grass and rock. For some reason, I just didn't want any part of that scene tonight, so I decided to go. My stomach growled loudly enough for the others to hear and a couple grinned.

"Guess you're still used to eating more, eh?"

I shrugged; I didn't want to sound like I thought I was better than them, but if they couldn't afford more for dinner than a donut, where'd they get the money for drugs? Or for that matter, for the parrot coloured hair dye and all the piercings.

They were headed nowhere fast, and were pretty content with that as long as they had drugs and the occasional donut. I realized that I didn't belong here any more than I did with Jeff. So I headed on out.

After a few minutes, I realized that I was being followed. It was the kid with the touch, slouching along like he thought I couldn't see him if he acted casual enough. I stopped to let him catch up, and he looked embarrassed at being caught. I decided he was younger than I'd thought, way too young to live on the street.

"How old are you?"

"Fifteen." He looked defensive and sulky, so I just gave him my best copy of my mom's 'I don't believe a word of it' stare, and he lowered his eyes.

"Twelve. But I'll be thirteen in a few months."

"Shouldn't you be home, won't your parents be worried?" I slapped my hand across my mouth as I realized that I sounded just like Miss Priss. Suddenly I missed white girl.

"Sorry, forget I said it. Let's go hang out in the mall for awhile."

He shrugged, as if it didn't matter what he did, and I set off. I tried to look like I was going somewhere specific, but considering my bruises and filthy clothes, I expected security to toss us out the moment they saw me.

Luck was with me though; we didn't see a single security guard. Not even when we spent a couple hours hanging out watching TV in the department store.

That's where I realized that I could never go home again. There was a news flash; a man was in the hospital with life threatening injuries from a knife attack. The police were looking for a dark haired female seen running from the scene. I knew they probably meant Carrie, but they might think I did it. I had the history with him; everyone knew how much I hated him.

What if they questioned Samantha? What if she told them about Jeff trying to... They would definitely believe I tried to kill him.

Maybe did kill him. The TV said life his injuries were life threatening and he was in critical condition. I wondered if my mom was sitting with him. Would she believe I tried to kill him? Does she hate me now? I imagined that now she'd be totally on Jeff's side. She'd never believe anything from me, there was no point even trying.

I decided not to go home; she'd just turn me over to the cops, who'd charge me with attempted murder. No-one would even be looking for Carrie. If they even knew about her.

So, where could I go?

I decided to ask the kid.

"Anywhere you want to go tonight?"

"I usually hang out near the bus station on Catherine. The lunch counter there throws out a lot of food when they close. You just have to beat the raccoons to the dumpster. And not be too picky, but at least the sandwiches are wrapped in plastic."

"A sandwich sounds really good right now. So, let's go." My stomach rumbled its agreement and the kid laughed, looking younger than twelve. I wondered how bad things were at home that he preferred the streets. Maybe he had his own Jeff to contend with.

CHAPTER EIGHT

Things get tense

Faraj

I sat at the counter of the sandwich shop down the street from the bus station. It was nearly seven o'clock, and if I waited until just after nine, I could save a dollar on the locker. They rented for a buck a day, always ending at nine at night. I figured that from here I could see if Fadi showed up, and signal him somehow not to go look at the locker.

I also worried about what I would do if the locker was already in use. But I supposed that they had allowed for that, since I was to give Fadi the key. I guess that any locker near six hundred would do.

I was scared, but kind of excited, like I was in a spy movie. I was Matt Damon with the whole world against me. But to be honest, I was starting to rethink the wisdom of taking part in anything planned by Ali. I just didn't trust him.

He struck me as the type who would kick a dog until it bit him, then demand the dog be shot for being dangerous. Or more likely, kick it until it bit someone else.

When the waitress came by, I asked for a menu. I had to order something; I couldn't go to a café to just sit for two hours.

But nothing on the menu would be Halal, so I had to be very careful. Blend in, but don't break the code. What the heck could I eat?

Aha! A toasted cheese sandwich. Perfect. And cheap, too.

An hour and a half later. My pop was getting flat and watery from the melting ice, and the waitress was starting to come over every five minutes to see if I needed anything else. I should have left, I was attracting attention. But I was still pretending I had a choice about going to the bus station.

I kicked at the backpack, and then had to reach down and put it back under the table. I struggled to pull my temper back under control. Having a tantrum would attract attention. But I really hated feeling helpless, and confused.

I mean, I wanted to be a part of something bigger, something to teach the West a lesson. Something... dangerous, and exciting. Something to make me a hero like my mother.

But now that my chance was here, I wasn't sure anymore. I don't even know what it is they were asking me to do, nobody tells me anything. They all just say to trust them.

I decided to look in the backpack. If the package was harmless, I'd deliver it like I promised. If it was something dangerous, but I'd pushed to be involved in something dangerous, hadn't I?

Then I saw that it was pointless to think about it. The backpack had a tiny lock through the zipper pulls. I couldn't peek inside if my life depended on it.

So, I had to admit to myself that I didn't really have anything to say about it. I had to deliver the backpack to the bus station. Let the cards lay where they fell, or something like that. Besides, I had promised Fadi that he could count on me.

Then I saw Samantha Hunter waking along Catherine. What was she doing here? Was it a sign? I tossed some money on my table and grabbed the backpack and left the café. I had to know why she was here, in case she knew what I was doing. Was there a leak in the group? Was there a spy? Was I being set up?

Samantha

By now it was getting dark and I was lost. I was starting to get scared, the area looked as bad as ours, maybe worse. There were warehouses, empty buildings, depressed looking blocks of apartments and a gas station. That looked to be it.

I decided that my life really, totally sucked.

I didn't want to go home, I knew how much trouble I'd be in; stealing money, smoking pot, wandering off without letting them know where I was going, the list was endless.

But I didn't want to be here either, wherever here was. But with no idea where I was, any move had an equal chance of taking me toward something familiar, or deeper into unfamiliar territory.

I wondered if anyone had ever died of exposure from being lost in Ottawa. Probably not at this time of year, it was still about fifteen degrees. I'd die of thirst first.

Oops, shouldn't have thought of that. Now I was thirsty and hungry. I'd have killed for a Coke. Or at least argued really loudly.

The street lights started clicking on, and I glanced at my watch. Eight-thirty. I was in trouble, alright.

I wondered if I should pray for divine intervention, maybe an angel or a star to show me how to get out of my life.

Then a miracle happened. Faraj leaned out of a door half a block away and called me over. What the hell was he doing here? Was he my angel?

Ashleigh

We cut around the back of the bus parking lot, and through a hole in the fence. The kid led the way between the buses, keeping us out of sight of the drivers hanging around the entrance smoking. We reached the dumpster in a remarkably short time, unnoticed and unscathed.

The kid clambered up the side of the dumpster like a monkey, and soon passed down a couple of slightly misshapen sandwiches.

"Those are for me, what do you want? I wouldn't trust the egg salad, but they have turkey and ham, and one roast beef."

"Turkey, and thanks." He grinned and ducked his head, embarrassed. I guess nobody ever said thanks before.

My sandwiches were handed down, and then he came squirming over the lip of the bin, jumping the last couple of feet to the pavement. He waved a hand toward the small patch of grass alongside the station.

"If we sit there to eat, we'll look like we just got off a bus and are waiting for our ride." I nodded; it would be nice to sit down to eat. This kid was pretty sharp. Maybe we could form our own gang. Look after each other.

Faraj

"Samantha Hunter!"

She looked at me, surprise written on her face. After a moment though, she walked over calmly, as if she'd known she was meeting me all along.

"What are you doing here, Faraj?" She sounded shaky and I wondered what she was doing here. I knew why I was here, but this was no place for her.

"Would you like something to drink?" She nodded and followed me back into the café. I knew I was avoiding answering her, but her presence would make me blend in, I had been hanging around looking worried because she was late.

I guess that was my answer, I had to follow my instructions. It was about twenty to nine. We'd have a quick drink then drop off the backpack at the lockers and go home. It was settled.

"So, why are you here, Faraj? I didn't expect to see anyone I knew this far from the building." She sipped at her pop, not looking at me. I tried to understand the question; we were only about ten blocks from home. Was that a great distance to her?

I decided to tell her only part of the truth.

"I'm here to drop off the backpack at the bus station. It's for a friend."

She nodded again, and I looked at my watch. Ten to nine, time to go.

"Are you in a hurry?" She'd noticed me checking the time, so I nodded.

"He's supposed to pick it up around nine thirty, but I can't wait for him. I was just going to stick it in a locker."

"How is he going to pick it up if you have the key?"

"I'll give it to him tomorrow, so he can pick it up." That sounded stupid, even to me. I was ruining it; she was going to know I was lying. But she just shrugged and stood up to go.

Samantha

Okay, so he was being evasive. It wasn't any of my business anyway, and I was way too happy to see him to pick a fight over it. I wasn't going to become a bag lady, lost forever on the streets of Ottawa after all.

So, Faraj dropped a five on the table, grabbed his bag and we left. We continued down the street in the same direction I'd been heading. At the corner I could see the big sign for the Ottawa Central Bus Depot.

Stupid! Another two minutes and I'd have known where I was. It was a good thing Faraj didn't know how scared I'd been, and I wasn't even lost.

The nine o'clock buses must all have just arrived; the parking lot was packed with people loading and unloading cars. Everyone looked so happy. Visiting friends, starting a new life, leaving the old one. Suddenly I wanted a bus ticket to anywhere.

It didn't matter where, just away from here, away from my life… away from me.

Faraj pulled open the glass door, and held it, motioning for me to go in ahead of him. Maybe he did like me after all.

At least until he could hear my mom screaming at me that I was a drug addict. Then he'd look at me with that scornful tilt to his eyes. That smile like he smelled something bad.

Shit. Even when something good happened, I could make it suck.

I tried to be happy, to concentrate on the fact that he had bought me a coke, and was walking me home. Maybe he could be my excuse for being late. I was keeping him company while he waited for his friend.

Ashleigh

"So, what's your name, kiddo? Mine's Ash." I figured that even though it was bad manners to ask questions, we'd had dinner together, and might be looking for a place to crash together. I should know his name. What if I had to ID him later?

"Mouse."

"Mouse? As in a small furry rodent?" Come to think of it, he was kind of mousey. Small bones, brown hair and eyes, Elijah Wood teeth. He grinned at me, as if he could hear what I was thinking.

"Suits me, doesn't it?" We both laughed at that. "My real name's Tommy, but no-one calls me that anymore."

I almost didn't hear him. Was that white girl and Faraj coming across the parking lot? What were they doing here?

I pulled Mouse to his feet and dragged him around the corner. Peering back at Samantha, I tried to decide if she'd seen me. It didn't look like it; she was staring around her like she'd never seen a bus station before.

Faraj had a funny, determined look on his face, like he was going to the dentist. I wondered if they were running away together.

"Who's that? Why are we hiding?" Mouse was trying to push under my arm to look around the corner too.

"It's my neighbours. What're they doing here?" I didn't see how they could have followed me, could they be eloping? White girl had never mentioned being involved with the raghead. But then, she wouldn't have, would she? Not with my referring to him that way.

"Do you want to follow them? See what they're up to?" Mouse seemed to be reading my mind.

I took his hand so we wouldn't get separated and walked into the throng.

Man, half the city seemed to be getting on a bus, meeting someone getting off a bus, or just hanging around the video arcade. What a confusing mess.

We tried walking straight through the centre of the station, but there dozens of line-ups, tickets, baggage check, loading passengers…

I couldn't spot white girl anywhere. I looked at Mouse and shrugged.

After I checked the ladies room, and the lunch counter, we wandered aimlessly for a few minutes. Then Mouse had an idea. Dragging me over to the benches along the wall, he hopped up on top of one to look around. Even on his tip toes he was barely taller than the crowd. I guess he'd forgotten that he didn't know who we were looking for.

A second later, he grinned sheepishly and jumped down. "Maybe you should look for them." He laughed infectiously. So, laughing, I climbed up on the bench.

From up here I could see over most people's heads. I wondered if it was a long weekend, which would account for how many people were travelling, but I couldn't think of one in late September.

Mouse tugged at my sleeve.

"The lockers and parcel pickup area are in the back, want to check there?"

"Good idea, maybe they're picking up something for white... Sam's parents."

So I hopped down and we held hands as we pushed, wiggled and inched our way to the other end of the station.

The whole station was kind of T shaped, with the public parking and bus loading zones on opposite sides of the long part of the T. The short end had lockers along both walls; another set of rest rooms, and the parcel pickup counter was along one end. At a glance, they didn't seem to be here either.

Where the hell did they go?

Faraj

I was grateful for the crowds at the bus station; they'd make it easier to disappear. If I was being watched, that is. Samantha still hadn't said what she was doing here, but since I didn't want her questioning me any further, I decided that I didn't care. She was cover, that's all. No-one would be interested in a spoilt white girl.

We pushed our way through the evening rush, and I wondered where everyone was going. What was so important that they rushed and shoved and cursed trying to get there?

Then Samantha asked me if I'd wait while she ran to the ladies washroom. I thought it a bit rude that she told me where she was going, but was glad that she'd be out of sight for a few minutes.

"Of course, I'll just put this in a locker while I wait." She nodded and started squeezing her way through the crowd.

I immediately turned to start looking for locker six hundred. I was near three hundred twenty, so I needed to go right. Nope, the numbers went down in that direction, so I needed to go left.

So, of course, a fat man in a suit was blocking my way. He was bent over, trying to jam three suitcases into a locker meant for two.

"Excuse me, may I get past you?" He glared at me for a second.

"There are plenty of lockers that way," he nodded toward the lower numbers. "So piss off, kid."

I smiled and moved away, but I didn't feel like smiling. Rude jerk.

I walked around him and down the line looking for the right locker. The row ended at five hundred fifty. What!?

I dashed across to the other side of the corridor, but the lockers there were all numbered over a thousand. Where were... then I realized that the numbers must start over back by the other end of the wall. Where I was before. Argh!

I hurried down the line of lockers; I didn't want Samantha to be with me when I put the bag in. Just in case there was anyone watching me. I didn't want them thinking that I had told her anything.

At last, locker six hundred. And it was empty. Quickly I threw in the backpack and started digging for change. I had been sure to leave a loonie out for this, so where was it? My watch got caught in the pocket flap on my pants, spilling change all over the floor.

I bent down to pick it up, and spotted the one dollar coin, half under the lockers.

CHAPTER NINE

The Big Bang

Samantha

I couldn't believe how bad I had to pee.

So of course, there was a line-up. I stood in place, trying not to jiggle, or bounce up and down. But I really really wanted to.

I must've looked pretty desperate too, because the woman at the front of the line turned to me as soon as stall opened up.

"Here, dear. You go ahead of me."

I grinned my thanks at her and raced into the stall, I was almost peeing myself. I heard someone object that I should have had to wait, but I didn't care.

The relief was exquisite. It was heaven. It was better than I imagined kissing Faraj would be... well, maybe not.

Then I remembered that I had actually told him I needed to pee. Suddenly I was so embarrassed. I couldn't believe I'd said that. He must think I'm a total dweeb. What kind of moron tells a guy she needs to pee on a date? Well, not exactly a date, but he did buy me a coke.

I came out of the bathroom, and turned in a slow circle. Somehow, I'd expected Faraj to be waiting by the door, like my dad did when I went to the washroom. But he wasn't around.

I was momentarily afraid that he'd left me. But I forced myself to calm down. I could find my way home from here; there were city buses that came by here, and maps of Ottawa at the information desk.

Then the crowd parted a bit and I could see Faraj. He was crouched by the lockers, feeling around on the floor. A feeling of relief washed through me, I guess I was more scared about being alone in this area than I'd admit. Even to myself.

I started toward the lockers just as a fat man shoved in front of me. I couldn't believe how rude that was.

Then the world ended. And it did end with a bang, just like Einstein said it would.

My eyes were open, but I couldn't figure out what I was looking at. I think it was a finger. But that made no sense.

My ears were ringing and everything sounded far away, like after a rock concert I was at last Canada Day.

I winced at the pain in my back. I felt like I'd been tackled by a football player, or three. I pushed my hair out of my eyes and came away with my hand wet.

I stared at it for a moment before realizing that my fingers were bloody. Oh God, I was bleeding.

The fat man had landed on me. It knocked the wind right out of me, and I could barely breathe in. How much does he weigh?

Shoving and wiggling and swearing, I managed to get him off my chest, though he still pinned my legs. But at least I could breathe again.

I levered myself up on my elbows, looking around.

What the hell had happened? People were thrown everywhere. The lockers looked like someone had hit them with a car.

Dust or smoke hung in the air making everything hazy and burning my eyes. I could hear people crying over the ringing in my ears, but couldn't tell where it was coming from.

A man beside me had pieces of sheet metal from the lockers sticking out of his chest. His breathing was strange and bubbly.

There was a woman in a short skirt, covered in black soot and red blood. She looked unreal. Like a movie zombie. She was trying to yell something, but couldn't catch her breath.

There was broken glass sparkling everywhere.

There was a fire over where Faraj had been.

Oh no, Faraj!

I started shoving frantically at the dead weight of the fat man, only to pause, thinking. It was dead weight. Was he... dead?

I managed to free one leg, and started pushing him with my foot. As soon as I was free, I'd start checking to see if people were alive. Starting with Faraj.

Then my conscience kicked in. I'd start with the fat tourist, and then look for Faraj. I'd check people as I found them, but I'd be looking for Faraj. He had to be okay. He just had to.

The tourist was dead. No question, definitely dead. He had no face. Just blood and smashed bones. I wanted to puke, but I was too scared. I couldn't breathe in.

I knew what had happened. I was so stupid not to see it coming.

Faraj was a terrorist. He'd bombed the bus station, just like those guys in London he'd talked about. Just like his mother.

Suddenly, my guts turned inside out and I threw up.

Fortunately, I didn't hit anyone.

I could hear a cell phone ringing.

I'm such a freaking moron! I should've called 911 to report this.

I have to do something, but I can't focus. My mind keeps wandering off on weird tangents. Why were there so many people here on a Thursday? Where is Faraj? Would mom be mad that I'm out so late? Why did he do this? Did he plan to kill me? Where did that woman get that gorgeous red purse?

Okay, focus.

Call 911. No, find a phone first. That cell phone that was ringing, where was it?

Where is everyone? Surely not everybody but me was injured. There must be an adult somewhere who can be in charge, so I don't have to be.

I just want to curl up and cry. I want my mom. Then the sprinklers kicked in. And the fire alarm went off.

I finally found Faraj.

He had been thrown across the hall from where he was before the bomb went off. That reminded me that he was the one who set it off, and I should be turning him over to the cops, but…

He's my friend. And I can't really accept that he's a terrorist. I mean, he's so cute. And polite. The terrorists on the news always look kind of crazy, and Faraj is just so normal.

It must be just a coincidence that he was talking about the London bus bombings.

Faraj was hurt. Badly, I think. I reached out to touch his poor face, and then realized how stupid that was. He wasn't my boyfriend (not yet, anyway) and he'd probably call me a whore again.

His leg was bleeding and had a piece of something sticking out of it. He looked pale and thinner that he did an hour ago. Like the pain was eating away at him, leaving only a shell behind.

Why am I getting all poetical now? I must be in shock, which would be why I can't focus. Why every time I try to think, my mind just wanders away.

Like right now. I grabbed my brain with both hands and forced myself to think.

Moving him would hurt his leg more. But not moving him meant that we both might get caught in the fire burning twenty feet away. Or choke to death on the smoke.

Also, the police would catch him. But if he did plant the bomb, then they should put him in jail.

Okay, first things first. How badly was he hurt?

By now Faraj was watching me. His huge dark eyes were glazed with pain, and he kept reaching for the shard of metal in his leg, then hesitating and pulling his hand away.

"Do you want me to pull it out?" I was hoping he'd say no, I was afraid I might puke again if blood gushed out. And if it had cut the artery, he might bleed to death. I saw that on CSI a few weeks ago.

But he shook his head no.

"Help me stand up, please. We need to get out of here."

So, I tried to. But he weighed more than I do, and being taller, it was really hard to pull him to his feet. He couldn't stand on the injured leg, and fell over again when he tried to. He pulled me over with him.

We ended up sitting on the floor, with me half on his lap. He kind of squeaked in pain, and fainted.

And the fire looked much closer. And felt hotter.

Where were all the grown-ups? All the firemen and paramedics and security guards and every body?

I was trying to drag Faraj away from the flames and toward the doors. I was holding him by the hands, but I was too short to get his head off the floor. I hoped I wasn't making a concussion worse, or breaking his neck, dragging it along the floor. It looked like the fire was going to beat me there.

It was getting harder to breathe without coughing and I was starting to feel dizzy. My eyes were watering so badly, I could barely see. Then I heard a wonderful sound. Fire trucks!!

We were saved. Abruptly, I found myself sitting down. Faraj was still unconscious, and piled awkwardly by my feet.

I stood up too quickly and sat down hard. That's no way to attract help, so I tried again.

"Over here, by the fire. Help!" I was coughing so much that my voice was sounding raw, but they heard me.

One of the firemen signalled the others and they headed in our direction.

I crawled toward the firemen, and one of them leaned over to pick me up.

"There's others. Over there, still alive." I gave up; I was coughing too much to make sense.

I let him carry me into the fresh air.

Ashleigh

Nope, they were nowhere. They just vanished. They hadn't had time to buy a ticket and get on a bus, so where did they go?

Maybe they just walked through the bus station to get to the bowling alley to the next street?

"You think they crossed over the parking lot to go bowling?" Mouse had read my mind. I grinned.

So we turned to the doors facing the bus lot, planning to cut across back the way we came. I more felt the whump of the explosion than heard it. I think I even felt the heat.

But all I knew for sure was that one minute I was walking toward the back doors, Mouse half a step behind me, the next moment I was lying on the floor, covered in shards of broken glass. And worse. Far worse.

Okay, most of it wasn't my blood. I couldn't decide if that made me feel better or not. Other people's blood all over me was kind of gross.

But at least I wasn't bleeding to death. I had about million cuts from flying glass, and my shoulder was bleeding where I got hit with a flying something. But I was mostly okay.

I wriggled over to where Mouse was laying. My knees still felt too shaky to walk.

Mouse was still unconscious. At least I hoped that was why he was so still. His face was so white.

I leaned over to listen for his breathing, but between the ringing of the fire alarm and the pounding of my heart, I couldn't tell if it was there or not.

I looked around the bus station, there was a fire going over by the lockers, and people were starting to cry for help. I couldn't help them, I couldn't help myself.

What had happened? Was it a gas explosion? Did a bus run into the wall of the station?

Oh my god, was it a bomb?

I crawled over to a woman who looked like she knew first aid. She was working on a man about her own age, and crying. She immediately begged me for help.

"What can I do? I don't know... I've never..."

"Put your hand here, and press down." She placed my hand over a bloodied cloth on his chest.

I could feel his rough breathing and there seemed to be air bubbles escaping under my hand. It would tickle if it didn't freak me out so much.

I could hardly hear her instructions over the fire alarm. But I thought she just said that she was going to look for something. What was I supposed to do? Just wait here with this guy dying under my hand?

Apparently so, she just kissed his cheek and left. I tried to say something comforting to him, but I realized that I was crying too.

"I'm not scared; we're going to be fine. It's just all the smoke and dust in my eyes." I didn't know if that comforted him or not, I didn't even know if he could hear me.

And shouldn't we be leaving? I mean, the place is on fire!
Where the hell did she go?!

I was really starting to panic by the time the woman finally came back. The fire was moving along the wall toward the nearest door, and the smoke was getting thicker.

She brought a paramedic with her. Thank God!

For the first time, I noticed emergency people rushing in. The flashing lights played over the broken windows, looking like flames.

We were going to survive.

I didn't even care if they arrested me for Jeff's attack. At least I was alive.

I think Mouse is dead, and I never found out who he really was. Will anyone miss him? What will his parents think when the police show up on their steps, sombre faces hiding their disgust for a couple who let their twelve year old live on the streets.

Would my mom hear about the explosion and wonder if I was there? Would she care after what happened to Jeff because of me?

I forced myself to look around. To see if anyone else needed help. Keep busy. Be useful. Try not to think too much.

Faraj

My mother used to have a saying about the more you try to hurry, the more you fall behind. It was certainly proving true today.

As I reached for the loonie to lock the backpack away, my fingertip pushed it further under the bank of lockers. I had to get down on my belly to peer under the edge to see if I could still reach it.

Then a huge explosion tossed me across the hallway and into the other bank of lockers. My head was ringing both from the blast and from slamming into the metal wall, but I could hear muffled screams and saw red.

Then I passed out.

Am I dead?
This unrelieved darkness didn't seem like death.
But it was silent as the grave.

After a moment I started to seriously hurt. Everywhere. So, I decided I wasn't dead.

But what had happened? Was it a terrorist attack?

A cold pit opened in my stomach, threatening to pull me in like whirlpool. Even my head spun as I realized exactly what had happened.

Ali had put a bomb in the backpack he gave to me.

And he had made certain I'd be here when it went off.

Ali had tried to kill me.

Or had it been Fadi? Was it his plan to have me deliver the bomb?

I had to get out of there before the police arrived. I needed to think.

Wait a minute. I wasn't alone. Where was Samantha? Did I get her killed?

I opened my eyes. I had to find Samantha and get away from here before the police came.

Oh, shit! My leg!

As soon as I tried to move, it hurt more than anything I've ever felt in my life.

I had to turn my body and pull my leg out from under me to see what was wrong with it. I figured it was broken, and worried about how much more damage I'd do by moving it. But I couldn't stay there. The police would never believe that I didn't know about the bomb.

I just bit down on my lip and grabbed my pant leg and pulled. It hurt so much I nearly passed out, but my leg did move to where I could see it.

There was a piece of what looked like the locker metal jutting out just below my knee. I tried to wiggle it loose, but it hurt too much. My head got all light and fuzzy for a moment.

Then I thought I saw an angel. Her brows furrowed with concern, her soft hands reached for my face... but why was she white, not dark like me? Shouldn't my angel be Arabic?

Then my head cleared and I saw that it's only Samantha Hunter. I was oddly disappointed, and embarrassed at the same time.

Ashleigh

The woman helped me outside while the paramedics carried the man out on a stretcher. She left me sitting on the curb by an ambulance to go hover over the man. I looked around; a lot of people were sitting around or being treated by the medics.

I guess a lot more managed to get out of the building than I'd thought. There must've been a hundred people milling around, their clothes ripped and dirty, faces slack with shock.

I thought of Mouse and was suddenly furious at all of these adults, who'd selfishly run for the exits, saving themselves while a little kid died.

I put my head between my knees and cried. For Mouse. And for me.

After awhile a medic came over to check me out. I guess I was okay, because she started asking me questions instead of putting me on an ambulance.

"What's your name, honey?" I didn't answer. I didn't care.

"Are your parents here?" I shook my head. "Do you want us to call them?"

I nodded and gave her mom's work number.

It was only after she left that I realized mom was probably at the hospital with Jeff. And she thought I'd stabbed him. She probably hated me.

CHAPTER TEN

Aftermath

Faraj

I awoke in the hospital emergency. A mask covered my mouth; cool flat tasting air flowed into my lungs. My throat felt raw, and my eyes still burned. But I was alive. I went back to sleep.

When I awoke again, there was a police officer standing at the end of my bed. My uncle stood behind him, looking furious and ashamed.

I wanted to say that I didn't do it, but I wanted to look innocent, so they had to mention the bomb first. I had to pretend that I didn't know what had happened.

Samantha

My mom and dad arrived at the emergency faster than I would've believed possible. They must've just flown.

They look so scared and happy at the same time. I felt like an idiot for thinking they didn't love me anymore just because I stole some money. Or because we weren't rich anymore.

It made me even more ashamed of my behaviour.

Ashleigh

I was sitting on a gurney in the hall, while they tried to contact my family. I could be here forever.

I looked around and noticed that quite a few people were stuck out in the hall. I guess all of the real beds in emergency were being used by more seriously injured people. Everyone in the hall seemed more or less okay, like me.

But others had their families rushing in. They were hugging and crying and kissing and I was alone. I wondered if that volunteer who asked for phone numbers had tried calling my mom yet.

Faraj

My grandmother had arrived and was praying in a high, shaky voice. I kept drifting in and out, like a tide. But my leg didn't hurt anymore.

The policeman was still there or maybe it was a different one, I couldn't tell. My brain was kind of foggy.

My uncle came back, followed by a man in a dark suit and a bad mood. The man came directly to stand near my bed, leaned down and practically growled in my face.

"Tell me about the bomb." I shook my head.

"What bomb? Is that what the explosion was?"

"You know damned well it was a bomb, you were seen putting it in the locker just before it blew. What happened, chicken out on committing suicide at the last minute?"

I shook my head again.

"I put books in the locker. For a friend."

"Like the books in your bedroom?" They had searched my bedroom! How could uncle Massoud let them? But I could see on his face, he believed them.

"A friend loaned me those books. I was just reading them, I don't agree with them." No, wait. I was not going to deny my beliefs to protect myself; I decided to tell the absolute truth. "Some parts of the books make sense, they are deeply spiritual. But other parts...."

"Who's the friend?"

"It doesn't matter; he wasn't involved in any bombing plot. He's a scholar."

"So you knew about the bombing plot."

"No! I was told to put books in the locker. That's all it was, books." But I didn't believe it, and neither did the suit.

"Who gave you the *books*?"

This was a struggle. I knew that Ali might have tried to kill me, but I did say that I had wanted to die for our people. And didn't I swear to protect the group, to help fight the oppression of our people?

But my heart said that Ali was dangerous. That he wasn't the one to lead our people, even the small group of believers here in Ottawa. He would give Fadi up in a second to save himself, I knew he would. And I didn't want to get Fadi in trouble; I didn't even know if he knew what Ali was doing.

But what if Fadi had planned it all? What if it was his idea to kill me by having me at the locker at nine o'clock? He did force the others to accept me into the group.

I needed time to think. And my head was still fuzzy from the explosion.

I wasn't going to get the time I needed to order my thoughts. The suit kept hammering at me, and uncle Massoud just let him.

"I agree with parts of the books, the spiritual parts. About keeping yourself pure and fasting and modesty and stuff. Not the parts about killing people."

"But you put the bomb in the locker. You were seen and identified."

"I thought it was just more books!" I was desperate for them to believe me.

"You attended meetings with known terrorists. You admit you delivered packages for them."

"If you know they are the terrorists, why are you yelling at me? You should be questioning them."

"Faraj, you will behave for once and answer this gentleman's questions." My uncle was blaming me for the yelling? I was trying to behave myself, but visions of Guantanemo Bay were starting to dance in my head.

Samantha

My mom wouldn't stop hugging me and crying. My dad just stood there, looking like he wanted to hit something.

"Mom, my hair's getting wet."

She sort of half laughed and half sobbed, and let go of me.

"What were you doing at the bus station? Were you running away?"

"I know things have been difficult lately, but…" They were both talking at once, and then they both stopped at once. We all laughed, but it was more to get past the awkward pause than because anything was funny.

"Mom, I wasn't running away. I was just…." Oh no, should I mention Faraj? Would I get arrested too?

"You were just what?" Dad was starting to sound angry, his usual way of dealing with worry. You're not scared if you're pissed off. That's his motto.

"Walking around, trying to think. Then I got lost by the Queensway." I decided to lie and say it was a coincidence that Faraj was there. I mean, it kind of was a coincidence. I didn't know he was going to be there.

"Then I saw the bus station and figured they'd have maps, so I could find my way home again."

"Why didn't you call us? We'd have come to get you." Mom sounded so reasonable, and saying it never occurred to me to call you sounds so stupid.

"I didn't want to worry you." Dad looked at me like I was an idiot.

"And you didn't think we'd worry more if we never heard from you at all?"

"I'm sorry, okay? I wasn't thinking, I was pissed off at you guys for always arguing and ignoring me, and us not having anything, or being able to do anything, or whatever. I just needed to get away for awhile to think."

"Let's not fight, not right now. Let's just be glad you're ok."

That's my mom, the peacemaker. Sometimes.

Ashleigh

I was lying on my back, trying not to think about Mouse when I heard a woman making a real ruckus at the other end of the emergency room. It sounded like she was taking the place apart. I figured it was the mother of someone who'd died. Or that woman I'd tried to help, if her husband had died anyway.

But as the noise got closer, and I could make out the words, it sounded like...

"Where the hell is my daughter?!"

"Ma'am, if you'd calm down..."

"You called me, you said she was at the bus station, so where is she?"

Mom?

"Madam, you can't just barge in here, someone call security!"

MOM!!" I started to get off the gurney, but my knee buckled under me. I hadn't even noticed it was hurt, but there was a huge brace on it now. I nearly fell, clinging to the bed side.

My mom threw aside the curtain sheltering me from the regular ward and strode through like a battleship at full speed. There was an intern kind of hanging off her arm, trying to slow her down and not having the slightest effect.

"Ashleigh!" I was crying, I was so happy and relieved to see her. She didn't hate me, she still loved me.

Then she slapped me so hard I fell to the floor, stunned.

"You little bitch! How dare you tell them to call me after what you did?"

"What? Mom? I…" I couldn't think, I was so shocked, my mind went utterly blank.

"Jeff is dead! Dead! You couldn't steal him away from me, so you… you…" She started to cry. Not for me. For that bastard, Jeff. I couldn't believe it.

"Mom, I didn't…. It was his dealer, Carrie."

She leaned in closer to me, and I flinched back. I couldn't help it.

"Don't you lie to me. You were seen running away. Don't ever talk to me again, you little bitch."

And she walked away. My own mother, just… walked… away.

Samantha

The nurse had come in and chased Dad out while she did all the usual tests: blood pressure, pupils, heartbeat....

Mom had remained, holding my hand. We were both silent until the nurse left.

Then mom looked at me with her serious face on. I knew this was going to be bad.

"Is there anything you want to tell me about Ashleigh or Faraj?"

Ashleigh? Why would mom bring her up? But better to talk about her than Faraj.

"No, what does Ash have to do with anything?"

"You weren't together at the bus station?" Why would mom think Ash was there?

"No. Ash was off with her native friends. I mean, I guess she was with them; she dumped me a few blocks from home and took off. Why?"

"Ashleigh was there, honey. She's been hurt, but not seriously. A little boy who was with her is dead. Were you with them? Do you know who he is? We need to call his parents."

I shook my head. I didn't see Ash there, and a boy was dead. I knew there must have been deaths, that fat guy for instance, but a little boy?

"What was Ash doing with a little boy? I thought she went to see Carrie." I didn't understand. Ash was headed away from me when she left, toward downtown and the Rideau Centre.

"What about Faraj? Did you see him there?" Shit. I'd hoped she wouldn't ask, but I guess someone might've noticed us together, and lying would be worse than the truth... well, probably in this case anyway.

"Well, yeah. I ran into him at the café where I stopped for a coke. But we split up when I went to the bathroom, why, was he hurt too?" There, that sounded innocent.

"The police say that Faraj planted the bomb. They say that CSIS is on its way to question him." She stared right into my eyes. "Did you know anything about that?"

"No! He wouldn't have. He's not like that. He's a really nice guy." Did I sound innocent enough? Did she know that I had suspected the same thing?

She kind of humphed, and continued to stare at me. I don't think she believed me. I tried to look more innocent, and realized as soon as I did that it was the wrong move.

"The police will want to talk to you. Don't lie and don't leave anything out."

"But mom, I didn't go there with him, I just ended up there by accident. Why would the cops talk to me?"

"Because you were there. And you know Faraj." She looked at the panic in my eyes and softened a bit. "I'll be here with you. Just don't lie to them; they're talking to everyone who was there. If you did something, trust me, someone saw you."

"But I didn't do anything." I was starting to cry like a baby, but I was getting scared. If they thought I had something to do with the bombing....

"Don't worry sweetheart, no-one's going to do anything to you. No cop in the city is big enough or mean enough to hurt you while I'm here."

I had to smile, that used to be her response when I was having trouble in school. And you know, there wasn't a teacher alive my mom didn't force to back off. No matter what they thought I'd done wrong.

Faraj

They were taking turns questioning me now. A huge beefy uniformed cop and the suit. My uncle and grandmother had been ushered into the hall.

My uncle had protested, I was a minor, not even sixteen until next month. But they didn't care, didn't listen.

I told them, you can't question me with out my uncle or a lawyer here. I have rights.

"Kadr was fifteen when he was arrested; you think they cared about his rights in Gitmo? You're old enough to kill people, then you're old enough to pay for it."

"But I didn't, I thought it was just more books. I'm innocent!"

I could see my uncle looking at me over the cop's shoulder as they shut the door. But I couldn't tell if he believed me.

A cop stood at the door, keeping my family out of the room.

I started to get really scared. I'd have to tell them about Ali. Even if it got Fadi in trouble.

The suit could see on my face that I'd come to a decision. He leaned in close and whispered how popular I would be in prison. No protective custody if I didn't talk.

"I'll tell you who gave me the backpack, but I swear I didn't know what was in it."

He just stared at me, like I was already dead.

"His name is Ali, Ali Faloul Saddique, the Mullah's son."

They just continued to stare at me, not saying a word.

"He told me to take it to the bus station and put it in a locker at nine o'clock. He tried to kill me."

Still no reaction and suddenly, I desperately wanted to just keep talking, tell them everything to fill the silence. But I held my tongue, waiting for a reaction.

Samantha

"Let's go over it one more time, just to get the details down." He bent down, making an eye contact that I couldn't break. "When did you first hear of the bombing plot?"

I couldn't stop myself. I rolled my eyes and moaned, "I already told you a billion times! I never did. If you don't know what happened by now, what makes you think you'll understand after a billion and one?"

My mom put her hand on my shoulder and glared at the sneering cop. At least she wasn't mad at me…yet.

"Can't we continue this some other time? My daughter's been injured and needs her rest."

"I'm sorry, Mrs. Hunter" But Constable Flynn didn't look sorry at all. "But it's best to do this while everything's still fresh in her mind."

Like I'd ever forget! This cop may have seen lots of dead bodies before but this was my first. I could still hardly believe it.

Four people were dead.

And Faraj….

Faraj was being questioned by CSIS. He would probably be arrested for the bombing, and all those people who died.

How could Faraj have done that?

I knew I was swinging back and forth on whether I thought he was innocent or guilty. The cop probably read that on my face and that was why he wouldn't just go away. But I thought I might be eighty percent sure that Faraj was innocent. Probably. I mean, he wouldn't have tried to kill me, would he?

Unless I was just one more stupid white girl, a good cover, nothing else. Maybe he had never liked me.

The cop was staring at me. I'd stopped talking, and didn't even know if he'd asked me a question or not.

Was he waiting for an answer, or just staring at me, waiting for me to continue? I didn't remember what I'd been saying.

"I'm sorry, my head is pounding and I'm kind of foggy. Can't you go away for a while?" I heard my voice shake with tears, and realized I was crying.

It was what mom needed to whip her into a protective bulldog frenzy. That cop was lucky she didn't bite him.

Eyes blazing blue fire, like lightning, she stepped away from me. Her closeness forced Flynn back a step, away from my bed. She looked like a cat stalking a rat.

"That is completely enough. You will leave, now."

"Ma'am, I have a right to question her..." Oh, wrong tactic. She hated being called ma'am, said it made her sound old and frumpy. I could feel her eyes narrow, the lightning becoming a laser beam, her shoulders squaring for battle.

Flynn backed up another step.

"Perhaps a brief pause for her to get some pain medication would be a benefit to both of us." He stepped toward the door, reaching behind him for the doorknob.

"I will call you when she's ready to see you again. I have your card. Sir." She sounded like an English noblewoman dismissing the help, her Rockcliffe accent coming out. The cop nodded and stepped out of the room, closing the door quietly behind himself. I could picture him shaking on the other side.

Yay, go Mom!

"We are not finished, Samantha. I want to know everything you didn't tell him." The laser eyes were turned on me now. Shit.

CHAPTER ELEVEN

The Next day

Ashleigh

The nurse said that I was going to be fine, and handed me a prescription for anti-inflammatories. Painkillers. Like these pills would kill the pain my Mom left me in. But I knew what would.

"When can I get out of here? There must be people who need the bed more than me."

"You'll have to wait for the doctor to sign your discharge papers. He'll want to go over your follow-up treatment with you."

"Great, go get him."

She smiled and left. And that was the last I saw of her or the doctor. After about two hours of practically climbing the walls, I mean I was so bored I wished I had homework to do, I gave up and left anyway. What was I waiting for? Someone to tell me how to take an aspirin?

As I wound my way through the crowds still milling around emergency, I wondered just how long I'd been there. Overnight, at least, what time was it now? I didn't see a clock on the wall anywhere.

A few people were waiting for the elevator, so I joined them. There was a discreet clock over the elevator, four-thirty. Almost twenty-four hours since Mouse died.

Since I failed that bright, shining boy.

I gritted my teeth to keep the tears in.

The doors swooshed open, and me and the others spilled out of the elevator to the main floor. I immediately pushed my way out of the waiting room to the street. I realized that I had no money for a bus and no idea where to go.

I bummed a few dollars off of people near the parking lot, out of sight of hospital security. For once I didn't make up a sad story, I just told them I'd been caught in the bombing, and lost my purse and backpack. Okay, I never had a purse, or the money they were glad to replace, but my singed hair and stitched up forehead really sold it.

I had about forty dollars by the time hospital security showed up, so I hurried to the nearest bus stop. I decided to let fate take me wherever I was meant to be. It turned out to be a number eleven, going right past the bus station.

I got off into a sunny, bright afternoon. There was still a haze of dust and smoke, the smell of burnt rubber and scorched metal in the air. There were still firemen and cops, though only a couple of each. A lot more men in suits and people with cameras were there. I guess they were like CSI on TV. I really hoped they'd found everyone in the wreckage, but I didn't see how. The entire short bar of the T shape had collapsed, twisted bits of metal rebar poking up from piles of brick and cement.

On the small section of scrubby grass between the sidewalk and the parking lot, an impromptu memorial was growing. I saw a few photos, people who had died, I guess. A lot of flowers, a few stuffed animals. I wondered if more kids than just Mouse had died. I wonder if they had found his family. I needed a newspaper. Now.

I looked for a garbage can, people always just threw papers away after they read them, but this time there weren't any. I guess no-one was really hanging around long enough to read a paper. I drifted back to the memorial.

I'm so sorry, Mouse. I wish I could've stopped this, saved you. Maybe never came here. But a small voice of common sense reminded me it was his idea to come and get sandwiches from the dumpster. For a moment I felt better, well, less guilty.

But would he have gone in if I hadn't wanted to follow white girl and see what she was doing with that terrorist bastard? No, he wouldn't.

I wrapped my arms around myself, the guilt and sorrow was strong enough to make my stomach ache. I was embarrassed to be crying, big, gulping sobs. I wished Mom had been more religious so I would know how to pray. I wasn't sure if I wanted to pray for Mouse or for myself.

Eventually, I wiped my nose on my sleeve and pulled myself together. It was supper time. It would be dark in a couple hours, and I had nowhere to go. Nothing to eat. No money to fill my prescription, and I was starting to hurt. I figured the pain meds from the hospital were wearing off.

Samantha

Mom kept me home the next week. I heard her yelling at the principal over the phone that she would keep me home to recover if she damned well pleased. It wasn't his call. And if he so much as whispered the words suspension or black mark on my record, she would destroy him.

Some days I loved my mom.

Other days were really hard. I'd had to admit stealing the money, and smoking pot with Ash. Now I was forbidden to hang around her, Mom was trying to set up play dates with my friends from the old neighbourhood. Not so easy when everything they wanted to do cost money we didn't have.

Dad said I was grounded until I was forty. Mom just glared at him like she thought he was making light of the situation, but he didn't look like he was joking.

I was getting screaming bored just sitting in my room or listening to lectures every time I went out of it. But I was starting to do the soul searching Mom wanted. I guess I was kinda spoiled.

Not as bad as she claimed, but maybe a little. But I didn't crash and burn like she claimed either. I only did weed the one time, and I wasn't sure I liked it. It sure sucked the next day.

I was still so confused by Faraj. He was still in hospital. His leg was really badly hurt, then got infected from the piece of locker. And he was still under guard so I couldn't visit him and ask what he was thinking.

Did he know about the bomb?

The question was driving me crazy. Did he try to kill me? Or was he hoping I'd be in the bathroom longer and be safe?

Faraj

I could hear the two police officers outside my door. They were discussing the hockey game last night, and flirting with the nurses. It almost made everything seem normal.

But it would never be normal again. My uncle and my grandmother believed the police, they thought I had meant to blow up the bus station. To kill seventeen people, including four children. How could they believe that?

Because I was still protecting Fadi and his group.

The drugs they were giving me for my leg made me too muzzy-headed to think about this properly. I couldn't get up by myself to go to the bathroom to splash cold water on my face to see if that helped, and the nurse just made me uncomfortable, wanting to help me in there. But when I had tried to do it by myself, I fell. They got really insistent after that. But at least they sent male nurses, well... a male nurse. I just prayed that he wasn't gay, considering how much he helped me. Was it a sin to let a homosexual wipe your butt?

I dragged my thoughts back to Fadi and Ali. I was sure that Ali meant to kill me, I remembered his smile as he gave me the backpack. His deliberate goading to make sure I went to prove him wrong. But was Fadi in on it? Did he know what Ali planned?

No, Fadi was my friend. He hadn't come to visit because he knew that the police would be looking at everyone who showed an interest in me. Or else he was under arrest, Ali would have blamed him. I knew it, he was corrupt.

The male nurse brought my supper tray. I was getting vegetarian meals because I was afraid to ask for Halal. They checked the nurse's ID, even though he had been in my room a dozen times today. It was meant to worry me, so I pretended it wasn't working. I smiled widely at the nurse, just so the police would see that I wasn't afraid. I pretended to be delighted by the bland, unspiced, overcooked food.

They waited until I had taken the lids off my dinner, but were too quick for me to get a single mouthful. The man in the suit was back, and he motioned for the police officer to remove my tray.

"There'll be time to eat later. First, I have some more questions for you."

My uncle tried to come in behind them, but the second police officer held him back. I could see that Uncle Massoud was getting angry at these strong arm tactics.

"I have retained a lawyer, he will be suing the police for this. You are preventing my nephew from getting his care. He was a victim, not the crook."

"Officer Dawson, remove him. And if that lawyer shows up, remove him too." He didn't sound like he believed my uncle, and really, where would he get the money? But it looked like my family did believe in my innocence, no matter what the police told them.

Suddenly I wanted to cry, just having them believe me made me feel so much better, and so grateful.

Maybe Uncle Massoud wasn't that bad after all. And look at what the more strict Muslims had gotten me into.

The man in the suit tasted one of my veggie burgers then put it back on the plate. He wiped his fingers and mouth on my napkin, and put it on my plate, as well. It was a deliberate insult and I tried hard not to react.

If I could restrain myself from reacting to Ali, I could do this.

Ashleigh

I was walking along Preston, smelling the Caribbean food truck when I put my hand in my pocket and found the money from the hospital. Wow, I must've had a head injury to forget that I had cash!

I turned and hurried back to the food truck, just as they were closing. The woman looked me over, and sniffed. But I was starving, so I decided to ignore it.

"What do you still have that's ready?"

"We're closed, girl."

"Look, I just got out of the hospital and I'm starved. I'll take whatever's easy for you to make."

"What were you in the hospital for, girl? Fighting? Drugs?'

"I was at the bus station yesterday when..." Without warning, my throat closed and I couldn't make a sound. I had been using Mouse's death to get money, and now sympathy so she'd cook for me. I felt so ashamed of myself.

"Never mind." I turned to go, I wanted to go where nobody could see me. I still wanted Mouse's real name.

"Wait, child. You were in that bombing? Where are your parents? You shouldn't be on the street."

"It's okay. It doesn't matter."

She glanced inside the truck at her partner and spoke softly in a musical voice. I didn't hear what she said, but it was pretty. I turned to go again.

"Wait child, you are so impatient. Sit here, I'll make you dinner. Do you like plantain?"

I turned and sat at the picnic bench beside the truck. Plantain?

"Isn't that the green flat leafed weed? Why would you eat that?"

She laughed, shaking her head.

"Different plantain, love. This one is like a banana, but not so sweet. Here, I'll make you some, and some chicken. You're too thin. You like rice?"

She was talking fast, like white girl. I wondered for the first time if white... Samantha was okay. She must've been close to the blast if she was with the raghead.

"Do you have today's paper? I'd like to read about..."

"Of course you would, here it is, love." Every time she spoke to me, she was more affectionate. Maybe she could adopt me.

I looked at the paper, front page, of course. And a six page special section inside. I took a deep breath and opened it to the first page of coverage.

Wow, I really was lucky to be alive, the photos of the station still burning looked a war zone.

The second page had a list of names. I was trying to get the nerve to look for Samantha when the woman came back with a coke and a huge plate of food. I only recognized the rice, but it all smelled incredible.

I was walking down toward home, more by habit than plan. I had kept the pages about the bombing. Sam's name wasn't there. I was so relieved. She was still alive. So was Faraj, but apparently under arrest at the hospital. He was expected to be formally charged as soon as he was well enough to leave. I was glad.

He was a killer.

I still had no idea what Mouse's real name was. They didn't have photos yet. Maybe tomorrow.

I was trying to think of where to go. Maybe Carrie would let me crash. I was headed that way anyway. Then I remembered what she did to Jeff.

I was surrounded by killers. But it wasn't the same with Carrie, she did it to protect me. But her place was probably a crime scene. And my mom had probably told the cops I did it, so I couldn't just show up.

I was stupid to even go to the bus station. Pure luck the cops hadn't recognized me.

Maybe I'd go back to the Rideau Centre. The Native kids would let me crash with them. I'd have to hide my money though.

And not let anyone know I was likely wanted or murder, they might turn me in for a reward.

My life sucked.

CHAPTER TWELVE

Coming together

Samantha

That CSIS guy arrived to talk to Mom and dad early in the morning. They made me stay in my room. I could hear snatches of the conversation, mostly my dad. He got loud at one point.

I thought that CSIS had decided that I wasn't involved, Faraj said that I was just a cover, to make him look normal. I couldn't decide if I was relieved or humiliated or angry. He never liked me.

I'm such an idiot.

As I was setting the table for supper, Mrs. Qahhar came to the door. She was hoping I could explain what Faraj had been thinking, but I couldn't help her. I didn't understand him, and he'd never confided in me.

She cried, they were talking about charging him as an adult.

I stood staring at the mirror while the tub filled. I was surprised to see I had a black eye. I knew about the stitched cuts along my eye socket. I should have realized it would go black.

I considered what it would look like when I stopped looking like child of Frankenstein. A scar would run along my cheekbone, under my left eye, curving up to meet my eyebrow. I also had two stitches closing a deep cut on my lip on the same side.

I turned my head back and forth. One side; normal. The other; child of Frankenstein. I decided that it made me look like a badass. Maybe I wouldn't get bullied at school anymore. Maybe I could rock this look, like a secret agent assassin.

I wondered if everyone at school knew what had happened. If they knew I'd been there. That I'd been with Faraj. That I had thought he was into me.

Ashleigh

I found them in their usual spot, talking about the day's take. It wasn't good. They were all hungry, low on weed, and surly. What little they had, they didn't want to share.

When one asked if I'd burned my hair with a lighter to look like I was in the bus station, I turned to go. One boy yelled after me that I should get a lot of money for that act, he wished he'd thought of it.

I felt dirty. I didn't belong anymore.

I walked around for a while before realizing I was headed up Somerset. I wondered if there was anything going on at the friendship centre. I might be able to sleep there, but it depended on who was there.

When I got there, they were just opening the doors for a movie screening, well, a documentary on northern reserves. Shelly was there, we always got along. She was white but her ex was Mohawk, she laughed that I could have been her daughter sometimes. It was a nice thought right now.

She just glanced up at me and asked if I wanted to check tickets at the door. Not a word about my hair or scrapes. I was so happy about that, I nodded and headed to the ladies to wash up and braid my hair.

I still looked like crap, but I was starting to feel better.

People didn't even start leaving until nine-thirty. There was tea and coffee, and everyone wanted to talk about the film. It was like they needed to talk about it. Finally Shelly started putting everything away, a hint to go home.

As I helped put away the kettle and the other tea things, she came over to stare at me. Like she was seeing me for the first time. But she just handed me the box of tea bags and walked away. Did she think I'd been fighting?

By ten I was starting to look at the closet in the break room. If I could hide in there without Shelly seeing me, I could sleep on the couch after they left. I might even be able to use the computer to look for photos of the victims.

But it was like Shelly was telepathic. No sooner had the last person headed for the door, then she called me into her office. To talk.

Shit.

Faraj

I don't know how I managed to fall asleep. One minute my mind was skittering in circles like bat trapped on someone's porch, the next I was awakened by yelling in the hall outside my room.

I recognized the cop's voice, telling someone to calm down and move along. Another man was yelling that "the murdering bastard deserves to die." He meant me.

I heard the sounds of a physical struggle, grunting, cloth moving, a slap of skin against skin.

My door flew open, and the cop and a stranger fell into my room. The strange man's eyes were red, his nose and cheeks high with colour. As he looked at me, his teeth clenched and his hands balled into fists. He lurched to his knees and surged toward the bed.

I was trapped, I couldn't move. My leg was still in a cast and held immobile by a metal cage. I cringed back into my pillow as the man reached for me.

But the cop was faster than I expected and grabbed the man, swinging him around and shoving him toward the door. Two nurses ran up and helped push the man out of my room. The cop turned and glared at me from the door.

"I should have let him have you. His daughter just died. That makes eighteen." He looked like he wanted to spit, but he just turned and left.

I lay back, wishing I knew what to do.

An hour later, the male nurse came in. He checked my pulse and blood pressure, looked at my IV lines. After a few minutes the cop shut the door, leaving us alone. The nurse immediately pulled out a piece of yellow paper and handed it to me. It was off of one of those message pads.

"You had a phone call."

It had no name or phone number, just a scrawled message to keep my mouth shut, or face the wrath of Allah. It sounded just like Fadi. His favourite line was "face the wrath of Allah" while talking about unbelievers.

He did know Ali planned to kill me. Maybe it was his idea, maybe he had never been my friend at all.

The nurse left me staring at the end of everything I had believed in.

CHAPTER THIRTEEN

Last words

Ashleigh

I perched uncomfortably on the edge of the chair. Shelley looked at me for a moment before reaching for the phone, but she didn't dial.

"Why are you here, Ashleigh? I know you were at the bus station, I can tell by looking at you. Why aren't you home with your mom?"

"She thinks I killed Jeff, she threw me out." My voice was a whisper. I had kinda forgotten that I might be wanted for murder. I really needed to read a paper.

She thought for a moment then dialled.

"Hello, Mrs Maracle? This is Shelly Wolfsong from the Ottawa Friendship... okay, I'm calling about Ashleigh," she paused listening. I could hear my mom's voice, high pitched with anger, but couldn't quite hear what she was saying.

After a moment, Shelly took the phone from her ear and stared at it a moment before quietly hanging up.

"You're right; she doesn't want you to come home tonight."

She bit her lip, staring at me like she'd never seen me before.

Holy shit, she thought I'd done it!

"I didn't kill him, it was his dealer!"

"Did you see him killed? Did you tell the police?"

"Yes, no, sorta. I saw her jump him, and she had a knife. But I was scared, so I ran." I was aware for the first time that I probably should have stopped Carrie. And I didn't want to rat her out, she did it to protect me. But Shelly was still staring at me, waiting for me. "I didn't tell anyone. I would've told mom, but she freaked out on me."

"We have to call the police. You have to tell them what you saw. And we need to find a place for you to stay."

"But the cops will arrest her. She only did it to protect me. Can't I stay here?"

Shelly took her hand off the phone and clasped her hands, watching me. She was clearly expecting an explanation.

The cops were pretty hard-core; they were wearing suits, so they weren't just regular cops. They were detectives. They kept talking to Shelly instead of me, and I wondered if I could sneak out.

And go where? I was kinda out of places to go.

Faraj

The guy from CSIS showed up fast after I told the officer at the door that I would tell them everything I knew. He told me that he had called my uncle, and that we had to wait until he arrived.

It was a very silent and very uncomfortable twenty minutes.

I started by telling him that I never knew there was a plot to bomb anything.

"I only delivered one other package for them, it was a book. Ali showed me."

"This is Ali Farouq?"

"Yes, he said that he was being watched, so he couldn't buy these books about true Islam for himself."

"And you believed him?"

"Yes. He said that the backpack was just more books for a friend to distribute."

He stared at me, his eyes flat and unyielding. I thought he didn't believe me.

"My brother's son is clearly a fool, but he not a murderer." My uncle was trying to help, I suppose I appreciated it. After all, I was a fool for listening to Fadi.

"Why are you suddenly so willing to cooperate?"

I showed him the note from Fadi.

"I thought he was my friend, but this is definitely from Fadi."

"You're certain?"

"Yes."

"What's his full name? Address?" I looked at my uncle, he just stared back, disapproving. He had never liked or trusted Fadi. I would be lucky to escape a loud round of I told you so.

The CSIS man stared at me until I met his eyes.

"Not until you promise to protect my family. I watch TV, I know you can hide them so Ali and his friends can't hurt them to punish me."

"You're in no position to demand anything. You'll be lucky not to end up in prison for life. Or on death row."

"Canada has no death penalty." I know I sounded disgusted with his lies, but I was serious. There was no way I would testify if it put my grandmother at risk.

"You know that for sure? You've read all the new terrorism laws?"

"I'll go to prison, then. Ali will know I didn't talk to you, so my family will be safe."

"You think he won't kill you in prison?"

"But he won't kill my family. That is my deal. Take it or leave it."

"Faraj," My uncle sounded horrified at my lippy response. "You are being disrespectful."

"Yes, I am. I will treat him with respect when you and grandmother are safe."

We worked it out, they would pick up everyone I had ever seen at Fadi's meetings, and charge them under the new laws. No phone calls, no bail, no one but their lawyer allowed to see them. It would have to do.

I still felt like I had betrayed my friends, my mother. But they had really betrayed me.

I had no idea what to do now. How could I just go to school like nothing was different?

Ashleigh

The cops were finally talking to me, taking me over it again and again. I finally stopped responding, and yawned so hard my jaw cracked loudly enough to be heard across the room.

"Tell us again why you were at Miss Whitehorse's apartment."

"Oh, God! I went to score some weed, okay? Jeff had nearly won, and my nerves were fu... shot. I just wanted to feel numb."

The two looked at each other and nodded.

"And Jeff was already there?"

Yes, for the thousandth time, he opened the door and we saw each other in the hall. Carrie knew I'd been trying to avoid my mom's boyfriend, but she didn't know it was him until he grabbed me."

"Then she attacked him with a knife?"

"Not exactly, he tried to grab my... breast, then she freaked on him. I had told her before that this guy tried to rape me. I'm only fifteen, she was trying to protect me."

"So why did she run?"

"Duh." I glanced at Shelly and shrugged apologetically. "She's a drug dealer; she didn't think you'd listen."

Shelly leaned forward and caught the lead cop's eye.

"Can't we speed things along? Ashleigh is obviously exhausted, and still injured from the bus station."

The lead cop looked me up and down, and nodded.

"We'll have to call Children's Services. If her mother won't take her back, she'll need to go into care."

"No!" I was not going into care. I heard things; there were worse men out there than Jeff.

"I'm registered with CS as an emergency placement for Native children. I'll just call my worker and leave a message."

I could stay with Shelly?

I felt hopeful for the first time in.... ever?

The cops nodded and got up.

"We'll file a report with CS tomorrow, and we will need to talk to you again, soon."

Shelly nodded, and grabbed her cell phone and tucked it into her purse. "I'll call CS as soon as I get home. The office is closed, so it won't make any difference."

Everybody filed out and watched her lock up the office, then followed her downstairs to lock the front doors.

I was going home with Shelly, and it was legal. It might be permanent if she was registered with CS.

She opened her door and made a hushing gesture as we entered the house. It was really nice, even with only the hall light on. I could see photos of her kids, a cat watching us from the couch, and a few toys scattered around. We didn't have any of those at home, this place looked a TV show.

Shelly walked through to the tidy kitchen, setting her purse on the counter and pulling out her cell. My stomach growled and she smiled, nodding toward the fridge. "There should be something in there you can eat, help yourself."

I could hear her leaving the message on her CS worker's machine as I stared at the full, even over-full fridge shelves. I had never seen so much food. I had no idea what to take. I saw a small plate on the bottom shelf, covered in clear wrap. I picked it up to see what it was; chicken leg, mashed potatoes, corn and peas. A real meal. Like a mother would make.

I swallowed hard.

Shelly took the plate from me and crossed to a microwave. As the plate spun, she poured me a glass of juice and pulled out a placemat and cutlery. She set me up at the table, then fetched my plate. Finally, she sat opposite me.

I put down my fork, she looked serious. How had I screwed up already?

"Ashleigh, go ahead and eat, dear." I put some potatoes in my mouth.

"Ashleigh, I'm afraid this isn't as simple as I made it look. We'll need CS approval for you to stay here."

She kept talking but I didn't really listen. She didn't want me either. The food was tasteless all of a sudden. And I wasn't hungry anymore.

Ashleigh," she hissed at me. "Are you listening? I need you to write out exactly what Jeff was doing, and what your mother said at the hospital. Anything she might have said that sounds like she knew what was going on."

"But she did know, I told her. That's why I ran away; she took his side when he denied it. She said I was just jealous, and I could see she'd never believe me."

Shelly grinned. How could she grin?

"That's great, sweetie. If you put all of that into your letter, I might be able to get full custody."

"Of me?" She wanted full custody of me?

She smiled again.

"You must be too tired to think, what did you think we were talking about?"

I just shook my head. This was unbelievable. I could stay here. In a real house.

With a real family.

Made in the USA
Charleston, SC
11 September 2015